OAKWOOD LIBRARY OF RAILWAY HIST

THE CROMER BRANCH

by

Stanley C. Jenkins, M.A.

THE OAKWOOD PRESS

ISBN 085361 384 2

Typeset by Gem Publishing Company, Brightwell, Wallingford, Oxfordshire

Printed by S&S Press, Abingdon, Oxfordshire

A view of North Walsham station looking towards Norwich on the 13th July, 1964.
Mowat Collection

Published by
The OAKWOOD PRESS
P.O. Box 122, Headington, Oxford

The Cromer Branch

Contents

A fine view of Cromer pier, photographed shortly after its completion.
Collection S.C. Jenkins

View of Cromer front looking east from the pier, *c*.1900. *Collection S.C. Jenkins*

Introduction

The 26 mile long branch from Norwich to Cromer is the only passenger line left open in North Norfolk. Promoted by the nominally independent East Norfolk Railway, the line was from the outset worked by the Great Eastern, and it eventually passed into full GER ownership. Opened, between Whitlingham Junction and North Walsham on 20th October, 1874, the line was pushed northwards to Gunton on 29th July, 1876, and on 26th March, 1877, trains started to run to and from the nascent seaside resort of Cromer. Cromer grew rapidly thereafter; new hotels mushroomed around the old fishing settlement, a sea wall was built, and the old wooden jetty was replaced by a fine Victorian pier. By 1897, the resort was so popular that a special new train – "The Cromer Express" – was laid on between Liverpool Street and Cromer. Headed by a Holden single, the train covered the 130 miles between London and North Walsham in only 158 minutes, putting Cromer within 2 hours 55 minutes of the Capital.

Cromer, at the heart of Norfolk's "poppyland", seemed to have an assured future as a popular (though rather select) holiday resort, but sadly, World War I heralded the demise of Cromer's Edwardian heyday, and, although the LNER revived through workings in the 1920s and 1930s, the glamour of the Edwardian era had gone for good.

The Second World War saw Cromer in the Front Line and, in those years of conflict, the branch carried large numbers of servicemen instead of the usual holidaymakers. The return of peace in 1945 was followed by a gradual build-up of holiday traffic – aided by petrol rationing, which staved off road competition. Shortly after Nationalisation, in 1948, a new named train, "The Norfolkman", started to run between Liverpool Street, Norwich and Cromer. In 1950, "The Norfolkman" was joined by the "Broadsman", and, with the re-introduction of the Holiday Camps Express the branch now carried no less than *three* named trains! The immediate post-war era was clearly an Indian Summer for the Cromer line, but with more and more people turning to alternative means of transport, and a Government which made no secret of its hostility towards the state-owned railways, closures and retractions were inevitable. On 20th September, 1954 the Great Eastern station at Cromer High was closed, and all trains henceforth ran into rival M&GN terminus at Cromer Beach. This was perhaps a long overdue piece of rationalisation, for Cromer High was inconveniently situated on the outskirts of the town. By 1964 the branch had reached its present form, with trains running from Norwich to Cromer Beach and Sheringham – a total distance of 30½ miles. Today, the line is worked entirely by dmus, and all stations are unstaffed halts – though goods services survive to Wroxham and North Walsham and the branch is, therefore, very different to the usual type of BR "basic railway", in that a significant proportion of its Victorian infrastructure remains intact.

In common with other Great Eastern branch lines, the Norwich to Cromer route has not, hitherto, received much attention from historians or enthusiasts, and it follows that this present volume is the first to be devoted exclusively to the Cromer branch. The line's recent history has, however, presented certain problems in that the present Norwich–Cromer–

Sheringham train service encompasses part of the Midland & Great Northern branch from Melton Constable to Cromer Beach, and for this reason it has been impossible to avoid at least passing mention of the M&GN. Similarly, the history of the Great Eastern branch to Cromer High is inextricably linked to that of the Norfolk & Suffolk Joint Line between Runton Junctions and North Walsham, and it has been necessary to include details of this linking route in order to tell the full story of the GER "main line". It seemed, on the other hand, that the East Norfolk cross country line from Wroxham to County School occupied a more peripheral position in terms of the Cromer branch, and to keep this present study within manageable proportions the County School line has not been covered in any detail. In essence, therefore, *The Cromer Branch* is a study of Cromer and its railways, with an emphasis on the former East Norfolk route and its important holiday traffic (including the lines to Sheringham and Mundesley).

The history of the Cromer line falls naturally into five periods, which have conveniently filled *Chapters 1–5* to form a coherent historical section. The following chapter contains descriptive information relating to the route of the Cromer branch and its physical characteristics – though it should be noted that the pace of change is such that one or two details in *Chapter 6* may be out of date by the time that this work appears in print. Moreover, the effects of rationalisation have resulted in the disappearance of many traditional features, and in an attempt to mitigate this problem, it seemed reasonable to include a chapter of miscellaneous details as an appendage to *Chapter 6*, in the hope that this section will be of interest to modellers or other individuals seeking greater knowledge of the pre-Beeching period. It is hoped, therefore, that *The Cromer Branch* will be of interest to railway modellers, as well as local historians, railway enthusiasts and other readers.

Stanley C. Jenkins

The Norfolk Coast Express at Cromer (*see page 45*). *J. Kite*

Historical Summary

Companies of Origin

East Norfolk Railway Company (inc. 23rd June, 1864)

Eastern & Midlands Railway Company (inc. 1st January, 1883)

Norfolk & Suffolk Joint Committee

Dates of Opening (passenger):

Whitlingham Jn–North Walsham	20th October, 1874	(ENR)
North Walsham–Gunton	29th July, 1876	(ENR)
Gunton–Cromer	26th March, 1877	(ENR)
Sheringham–Cromer	16th June, 1887	(E&MR)
North Walsham–Mundesley	1st July, 1898	(N&SJ)
Mundesley–Runton	23rd July, 1906	(N&SJ)

Dates of Closure to passengers

Roughton Road Jn–Mundesley	6th April, 1953
Cromer Jn–Cromer High	20th September, 1954
Mundesley–North Walsham	3rd October, 1954

Distances

Norwich–Cromer High	23 miles 79 chains
Norwich–Cromer Beach	26 miles 54 chains
Norwich–Sheringham (BR)	30 miles 40 chains

Mode of Operation (pre-1954):

Double track Whitlingham Jn–North Walsham; single line North Walsham–Cromer Junction with crossing loop at Gunton; double track Cromer Junction to Cromer High. Single track between Cromer Beach and Sheringham with passing place between Runton East and West Junction.

Mode of Operation (present day):

Double track Whitlingham Junction–Wroxham; single track Wroxham to Sheringham with crossing loop at North Walsham and passing place for dmu stock at Cromer Beach.

Typical Motive Power:

'D13', 'D15', 'D16/2' and 'D16/3' 4–4–0s, 'B12' and 'B17' 4–6–0s, 'J15' and 'J17' 0–6–0s, 'F3' and 'F4' 2–4–2Ts, class '31' A1A–A1As, class '101' dmus.

Acts of Parliament

ENR 1864 (27 & 28 Vic. cap. 122): incorporation
ENR 1869 (32 & 33 Vic. cap. 92): additional time
ENR 1872 (38 & 39 Vic. cap. 17): deviations, additional time for purchase of land and extension to Cromer.
ENR 1878 (42 & 43 Vic. cap. 36): extension from Wroxham.
ENR 1879 (43 & 44 Vic. cap. 136): extensions.

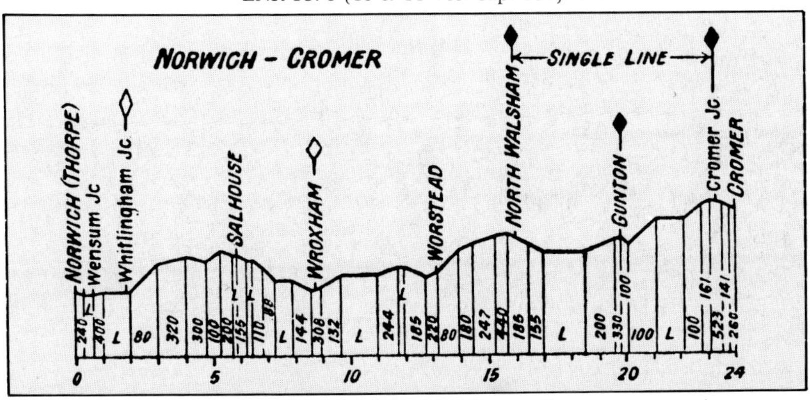

Gradient profile of the GER line to Cromer.

Cromer, looking west towards the church and pier, at the turn-of-the-Century. Note the bathing machines and the Cromer "lugger" (*right*). *Collection S.C. Jenkins*

Looking west towards Cromer church (before the erection of the pier); this view probably dates from around 1890. *Collection S.C. Jenkins*

Chapter One

Origins, Opening and Early Years (1864–1882)

Situated in a remote position on the picturesque, but little-visited north Norfolk coast, pre-railway Cromer was a tiny settlement with a population (in 1801) of only 676. In earlier times, the area was said to have been heavily-populated, but coastal erosion was a major problem, and in the reign of Henry IV the township of Shipden was swallowed by the encroaching North Sea, leaving the neighbouring parish of Cromer in splendid isolation above the relentless waves.

The size of Cromer's parish church suggests that, in Medieval times, the town had been a place of some importance, but in later years, the townsfolk eked out a meagre existence as fishermen. The fishing craft used locally were black-sailed luggers, and in the mid-Victorian period these simple vessels were used mainly for crab and lobster fishing – though some larger boats ranged farther afield in search of cod or herring. (The crab season lasted from April to June, and thereafter the men fished for lobsters).

Despite the importance of its fishing fleet, Cromer was poorly-equipped as a seaport; indeed, there was no harbour of any kind, and vessels loaded and unloaded their cargoes alongside an exposed wooden jetty. Under these circumstances, storms presented major problems, and many of Cromer's fishing vessels were in fact based at nearby Blakeney. In 1845, Cromer's jetty was severely damaged by a storm, and thereafter coal and other types of cargo were unloaded on the beach – a hazardous operation which involved the vessels concerned beaching themselves at high tide.

Apart from coastal transport, Cromer and neighbouring towns such as North Walsham and Wroxham were served by a relatively complex system of navigable waterways, including the River Bure and River Ant. There was, in addition, the North Walsham & Dilham Canal – a man-made waterway, opened in 1826 and built partly at the expense of Lord Suffield of Gunton Park. These waterway links were supplemented by various stage coach and carrier services providing a slow (but surprisingly comprehensive) network of services in and around Norwich.

Early Railway Development

Although East Anglia was a somewhat remote area, it had never been regarded as a backward region; on the contrary, the efforts of improving landlords such as Thomas Coke of Holkham (1752–1842) ensured that Norfolk and Suffolk were frequently in advance of other areas. Moreover, East Anglia had, since the Reformation, been a staunchly Protestant region with a long tradition of thrift, sobriety and hard work, and East Anglians had, not surprisingly, achieved prominence in many walks of life – particularly banking, farming and the Royal Navy (Nelson, of course, was a Norfolk man, while Admiral Vernon and Captain Broke came from Suffolk).

Inevitably, the rapid development of railways in other parts of the country led to demands that this new and revolutionary form of transport should be brought to East Anglia, and as early as the 1820s there were plans for a line linking Norwich or Cambridge to London. In 1821, for instance, the pioneer railway promoter William James (1771–1837) had surveyed a possible "engine railroad from Bishops Stortford to Clayhithe Sluice with a branch to Waddon", while in 1824–25 an equally-grandiose "Norfolk, Suffolk & Essex Railroad" was suggested. If successful, this last-named scheme would have provided a useful rail link between Yarmouth, Norwich and London which could, at a later date, have formed a viable nucleus for future railway development.

These 1820s projects were hopelessly premature, but tangible progress was made in the following decade, and on 4th July, 1836 two important schemes – the Eastern Counties Railway and the Northern & Eastern Railway – received the Royal Assent.

The Eastern Counties Railway was, in effect, a revival of the earlier Norfolk, Suffolk & Essex scheme, and like its abortive predecessor, the company hoped to link Yarmouth, Norwich and London. Plagued by financial and other problems, the Eastern Counties Railway was unable to fully implement its original scheme, but by 29th March, 1843 a much shorter line was in operation between London and Colchester.

Meanwhile, a separate company – the Yarmouth & Norwich Railway – had made good progress with its own line to Norwich, and when opened to traffic on 1st May, 1844 this short line became the very first steam railway in Norfolk.

Further west, the Northern & Eastern Railway had also made good progress, and a line between London and Bishops Stortford was in operation by 1842. On 1st January, 1844, the Eastern Counties Railway (which had still not progressed beyond Colchester) took over the Northern & Eastern on a 999 year lease, and on 29th July, 1845 the Northern & Eastern was extended to Cambridge and Brandon. At Brandon, this new line met a branch from Norwich, the two lines being opened simultaneously in order to complete a chain of railways between London, Cambridge and Norwich. In a further development, the Norwich & Brandon Railway joined forces with the Yarmouth & Norwich to form the aptly-named Norfolk Railway, and by 15th December, 1845 the Yarmouth & Norwich and Norwich & Brandon lines had been physically-linked to complete a continuous line of communication between Yarmouth, Norwich and London.

Railway schemes were, by this time, coming thick and fast, for the 1840s were a time of "Railway Mania" in which companies were floated in an uncoordinated and sometimes reckless manner. Lines promoted during this period of furious expansion included the Lynn & Ely, the Lynn & Dereham, the Lynn & Fakenham, the Eastern Union, the Newmarket & Chesterford, the Waveney & Great Yarmouth and the Wells to Thetford. Of greater significance, as far as North Walsham and Cromer were concerned, was a proposed "North of Norfolk" railway which would have linked Norwich, Cromer and Holt. Unfortunately, Britain was, in 1845, heading towards an economic crisis of unparalleled dimensions, and in the event, the North of Norfolk – and many other lines projected during the Railway Mania – were doomed to inglorious failure.

By 1847 the British people were investing far more money in railways than they could possibly earn from the export of manufactured goods, and on top of this, a series of failed harvests culminated in the great famines of 1846, 1848 and 1849 – which led, in turn, to riots and revolutions throughout Europe. In these grave and unhappy circumstances the Railway Mania was followed by a stock market crash, and against this background of disaster many wild schemes hatched during the "Mania" years were abandoned.

Other, more soundly-based projects were rushed to completion, and in these years several important sections of line were opened to traffic – among them the Eastern Union between Colchester and Ispwich (15th June, 1846), the Ipswich & Bury between Ipswich and Bury St Edmunds (24th December, 1846), and an Eastern Union extension from Haughley to Norwich (12th December, 1849).

Many lines promoted during the 1840s were so small that they could not remain viable as independent concerns, and for this reason they tended to look towards amalgamation as an answer to financial or operational problems. Inevitably, small companies such as the Norfolk Railway gravitated towards larger, more successful concerns, and in this way the Eastern Counties gradually assumed a position of undisputed power throughout East Anglia. In 1848, for example, the Eastern Counties Railway became responsible for the day-to-day running of the Norfolk Railway, and with both the Yarmouth–Norwich–London *and* Norwich–Cambridge–London lines under Eastern Counties control, it seemed likely that any future extensions to North Walsham or beyond would be constructed by, or with the acquiescence of, the Eastern Counties company.

Formation of the East Norfolk Railway

There had, in the interim, been further proposals for a line running beyond the existing railhead at Norwich – among them a suggested "East Norfolk" line serving both Aylsham and Cromer. In 1859 a public meeting was called to discuss this proposed railway, and although the East Norfolk scheme was not immediately successful, the idea of a railway to North Walsham was immensely attractive to landowners such as Lord Suffield (1830–1914), who saw the railway as a means of improving local agriculture. Lord Suffield, who farmed about 12,000 acres in north Norfolk, soon emerged as a leading supporter of the East Norfolk proposal and in the next few months he was able to consolidate support for the scheme among his fellow-landowners.

Several more public meetings took place during the early 1860s, and as a result of these meetings it was agreed that an approach would be made to Parliament with the aim of building a short branch from Norwich to the market town of North Walsham. Such a line would stimulate residential development in nearby Cromer, but it seems that, in the short term, the East Norfolk promoters were more interested in providing improved transport facilities for local farmers and serving the transport needs of North Walsham (then a small town of about 2,900 inhabitants, with a brewery, maltings and other small industries which would benefit from the provision of new transport links).

Meanwhile, the process by which the Eastern Counties Railway had acquired control of its smaller, weaker neighbours was culminating in what was perhaps a long-overdue amalgamation, and on 7th August, 1862, an Act to "Amalgamate the Eastern Counties, the East Anglian, the Newmarket, the Eastern Union and the Norfolk Railway companies" received the Royal Assent.[1] Although in effect the Eastern Counties had simply absorbed lines that it already worked, the company wisely decided to restyle itself "The Great Eastern Railway" – thereby establishing in the public eye an entirely new organisation which would not be tainted with the ECR's unfortunate reputation for poor timekeeping and bad management.

The newly-created Great Eastern Railway showed considerable interest in the proposed East Norfolk line, and when the ENR Bill was submitted to Parliament in the early part of 1864 the scheme was fully supported by the GER – which had already agreed to work the completed branch in return for a share in the gross receipts.

On 9th February, 1864 *The Journal of the House of Commons* reported that the Great Eastern company (and certain individual promoters) had petitioned Parliament "for leave to bring in a Bill for the making of Railways from the Great Eastern Railway to North Walsham and Horstead in the county of Norfolk and for other purposes". The petition was presented and read, and the ENR Bill was "ordered to be brought in ... by Colonel Coke and Mr. Gurdon" on that same day.[2] The East Norfolk Bill was read for the first time on 11th February, and then "ordered to be read a second time". Thereafter, the Bill passed relatively smoothly through the House of Commons and was subsequently passed to a Lords Committee for further scrutiny. This was, however, a mere formality, and in spite of opposition from the North Walsham & Dilham Canal it seemed that the ENR Bill was likely to have an easy passage.

A few days later Lord Redesdale (himself an important railway shareholder with significant interests in the GWR) reported that the East Norfolk Bill was all in order apart from a clause prohibiting the installation of level crossings.* It was felt that this provision was unnecessary because the proposed branch line "traversed a level agricultural district with no very large traffic" and there was no reason why level crossings should not be allowed at specified points in the parishes of Great Plumstead, Little Plumstead, Hovetone St Peter, Tunstead, Worstead, Rackheath and Sloley.[3]

On 20th June the House of Commons proceeded to "take into consideration" the Lords' amendment, and thereafter the clerk was ordered to "carry the Bill up to the Lords and acquaint them that the House had agreed to the amendment". This being done, the Act "for making a railway from the Great Eastern Railway to North Walsham" received the Royal Assent on 23rd June, 1864.[4]

The East Norfolk Act (27 & 28 Vic. cap. 122) provided for the construction of a 14 mile railway from Whitlingham Junction, on the former Yarmouth & Norwich section of the GER, to the town of North Walsham. Capital of £88,000 in £10 shares was authorised, together with loans of £23,000; a time limit of five years was set for completion of the works, and the number of Directors would be nine. The ENR company was authorised to enter into

* In fact all level crossings were frowned upon by the Board of Trade, and Parliament had to give special authorisation for such crossings to be installed.

working agreements with the Great Eastern, and the GER was allowed to subscribe for up to £29,300 worth of East Norfolk share capital. Moreover, the Great Eastern, having subscribed for ENR shares and become a shareholder in that undertaking, was permitted to nominate East Norfolk Directors to vote on its behalf at ENR meetings.[5]

The first meeting of the newly-constituted East Norfolk Railway was held at Norwich in September 1864, and those present at this inaugural gathering heard Lord Suffield complain, with a hint of exaggeration, that "strenuous opposition had been offered" to their entirely praiseworthy scheme. Despite these objections, the Bill had passed successfully through Parliament, and in an atmosphere of growing enthusiasm, the East Norfolk Chairman reported that the company's Engineer had already been instructed to "lay out the line" to North Walsham; indeed, continued the Chairman, there was "every reason" to hope for an early continuation of the railway from North Walsham to Cromer.[6]

The next speaker was Lord Wodehouse who, in moving the adoption of the report, explained that a short branch to Horstead had been rejected by the Commons; however, this line was not a "material part of the scheme", and he considered that "speaking generally, the application to Parliament had been an entire success". Lord Wodehouse then said a few words about his own involvement with the East Norfolk scheme; like Lord Suffield, he was an important supporter of the company, but being resident in London for much of the time he would not be able to serve on the East Norfolk Board – though he would be "exceedingly glad to give every possible assistance to the company".[7]

Lord Wodehouse's resignation left a vacancy on the ENR Board, but it seems that a replacement had already been found, and Mr H. Chamberlin was immediately appointed in his place. The East Norfolk promoters had apparently organised themselves as Directors *before* the first public meeting in September; however, the assembled shareholders voiced no objections to this arrangement, and with Mr Chamberlin's appointment the nine-man Board of Directors was complete. Lord Suffield was an obvious choice for the position of Chairman, and the other Directors included Sir J.H. Preston, William Henry Trafford, Robert Blake Humfrey, and Edward Leathes, together with James Goodson, H.J.W. Jervis, and Jonah Smith Wells who sat on the ENR Board as representatives of the Great Eastern Railway.[8]

Construction and Opening

Having obtained their Act and organised themselves into a properly-constituted Board of Directors, the East Norfolk promoters were eager to begin construction. The authorised route ran due north from Whitlingham Junction, and with few physical obstacles to impede the work, it was expected that rapid progress would be made.

Building operations were under way by 1865, and it seemed at the time that the East Norfolk branch was destined for early success. Unfortunately, external events intervened before the project could be brought to fruition, and in May 1866 the sudden failure of bankers Overend & Gurney precipi-

AN

ACT

To authorize the Extension to Cromer of the East Norfolk Railway, and an alteration of that railway, and to give further time for the compulsory purchase of lands for that railway, and for its completion, and for other purposes affecting the East Norfolk Railway Company and the Great Eastern Railway Company.

[ROYAL ASSENT 27TH JUNE 1872.]

WHEREAS by " The East Norfolk Railway Act 1864 " (in this Act called The original Act) the East Norfolk Railway Company (in this Act called "The Company") was incorporated with a capital of eighty-eight thousand pounds in shares of ten pounds each and with power to borrow on mortgage any sum not exceeding twenty-nine thousand three hundred pounds and was authorized to make and maintain a railway from the Norwich and Yarmouth line of the Great Eastern Railway in the parish of Thorpe next Norwich to North

Preamble 27 & 28 Vict. c. 122.

The front page of the Act authorizing the Extension to Cromer.

East Norfolk Railway.

Walsham and (section 4) their undertaking was directed to be called "The East Norfolk Railway."

And whereas by the original Act (section 11) it was enacted that the number of the directors should be nine:

32 & 33 Vic. c. 92.

And whereas by the original Act (section 19) the time allowed for the exercise of the powers by that Act conferred for the compulsory purchase of lands was limited to three years and (section 20) the time allowed for the completion of the railway was limited to five years from the passing of that Act but by "The East Norfolk Railway Act 1869" (which received the royal assent on the twelfth day of July one thousand eight hundred and sixty-nine) (section 4) the time allowed for the completion of the railway was extended to three years after the passing of the last-named Act. But the time allowed for the compulsory purchase of lands was not extended:

And whereas by the original Act (section 32) the Company and the Great Eastern Railway Company were authorized to enter into agreements with respect to the maintenance and management of the railway by that Act authorized or any part thereof and of the works or any of them connected therewith the use and working of the said railway or any part thereof and other matters and (section 34) the Great Eastern Railway Company were authorized to subscribe for take and hold shares or stock in the capital of the Company to any extent not exceeding twenty-nine thousand three hundred pounds:

And whereas by the original Act (section 36) it was enacted that the Great Eastern Railway Company on becoming and while continuing under the powers of that Act shareholders in the undertaking might from time to time appoint one of the directors nominated by the Great Eastern Railway Company as thereinafter provided (whether such director should hold shares in the Company or not) to vote on their behalf at meetings of the Company and that the Great Eastern Railway Company might from time to time revoke any such appointment and appoint any other of such directors on their behalf:

And whereas there is no provision in the original Act for

2

tated an economic crisis of major proportions, resulting in unemployment, riots and civil disorders throughout the country. Panic shook the City, and with individuals and companies facing ruin, small companies such as the East Norfolk Railway found it increasingly difficult to raise their authorised capital. For three months the bank rate rose to ten per cent, and in these crisis conditions the original 1864 East Norfolk scheme almost foundered.

It seemed that the projected North Walsham branch would never be completed, and matters were not helped by the death of the original contractor, who had also been an important supporter of the scheme. Eventually, improved trading conditions enabled the promoters to resurrect their project, but there had, in the meantime, been a significant change of plan, and as well as serving Wroxham, Worstead and North Walsham, the revived East Norfolk line would also carry holiday traffic to and from the nearby coastal town of Cromer. This was, on the face of it, an excellent idea, and in fact the promoters had always intended to extend their line northwards to the coast at the very first opportunity.

Seaside towns were, by the 1860s and 1870s, springing up on all parts of the coast, and Lord Suffield and his fellow-Directors were clearly aware of the immense success of neighbouring Hunstanton – where an entire resort had been planned and built by the promoters of the Lynn & Hunstanton Railway Company. (See *The Lynn & Hunstanton Railway* by S.C. Jenkins).

Confident that the spectacular success of the Hunstanton branch could be repeated, the East Norfolk Directors resumed construction of their own line, though in 1868 it was reported that the line would be built, in the first instance, only as far as Wroxham.[9]

On 12th July, 1869 the company obtained a new Act (32 & 33 Vic. cap. 92) granting additional time for completion of the works, and on 27th June, 1872 it was necessary to obtain a further Act (38 & 39 Vic. cap. 17) authorising an "extension to Cromer" and an extension of time for the compulsory purhase of lands. The 1872 Act also permitted certain deviations of the authorised route between Whitlingham Junction and Cromer.[10] At the same time, there was an attempt to clarify the relationship between the East Norfolk and Great Eastern Companies, and the new Act referred to "agreements with respect to the maintenance and management of the railway" that the two companies had been authorised to enter into under the provisions of the original 1864 Act.

Having obtained these additional Acts the East Norfolk company was, at long last, able to make some progress with the work of construction, and in the ensuing months the railway started to take tangible shape in the pleasant Norfolk countryside. With building operations under way, the railway press started to take an interest in East Norfolk affairs, and on 22nd February, 1873 *The Railway Times* printed this brief report of a recent ENR general meeting:

> EAST NORFOLK RAILWAY – The report states that an offer has been received from Messrs Lucas to construct the works from the Great Eastern at Thorpe to North Walsham. The Directors, considering the terms satisfactory, have, subject to the approval of the shareholders, accepted the offer, as it guarantees the completion of the line without delay. £44,277 has been received on capital account, and £34,220 has been expended, leaving a balance of £10,057. The length of railway authorised to be constructed is 22¼ miles.

Events were now moving towards a successful completion of the East Norfolk scheme, and as the pace of construction quickened, the people of Salhouse, Wroxham and Worstead – many of whom would never have *seen* a railway let alone travelled on one – were able to study the new form of transport in greater detail. The first engineering trains were probably in use on temporary contractor's tracks during the summer of 1873, and by analogy with other contracts, Lucas Brothers are likely to have employed small Manning Wardle (or similar type) saddle tanks to remove spoil from cuttings and tip material to form the new embankments.

The works were substantially complete by the summer of 1874, and on Tuesday 20th October, 1874 the line was opened for passenger traffic between Whitlingham Junction and North Walsham, a distance of fourteen miles. Intermediate stations were provided at Salhouse, Wroxham and Worstead, and all train services were provided by the Great Eastern Railway in return for a share of the gross traffic receipts.

The opening was reported in considerable detail by *The Railway Times*, and on Saturday 24th October, 1874 this influential shareholders' journal printed an informative first-hand description of Opening Day:

> EAST NORFOLK RAILWAY – This line, from Norwich to North Walsham which has been about ten years in construction, was opened for traffic on Tuesday. There are stations at Whitlingham Junction, where the line leaves the Norwich and Yarmouth line of the Great Eastern system, Salhouse, Wroxham, Worstead and North Walsham. The line, which was constructed by Messrs Lucas Brothers, will be worked by the Great Eastern, which holds the greater part of the share capital. The run from Norwich to North Walsham will be made over the new line in about forty minutes.
>
> The first train left North Walsham at 6.15 in the morning for Norwich, and during the day five trains each way were run from North Walsham. The distance is sixteen miles, and there are five stations. The agricultural district covered by the extension is one of the richest in the eastern counties. The terminus at North Walsham is in close proximity to the town.

The new railway crossed undulating, rather than flat terrain, but there were no major earthworks, and the only engineering feature of note was a small bridge across the River Bure at Wroxham. Elsewhere, the line was carried on embankments or through cuttings for much of its length, and there were several over and underbridges, together with numerous level crossings at the southern end of the line, and between Wroxham and Worstead. Generally speaking, however, the East Norfolk route had less level crossings than many other East Anglian lines, and in this respect it was a better-engineered route than some of its contemporaries. The branch was, on the other hand, severely-graded by Norfolk standards, with a mile long, rising gradient of 1 in 80 near Whitlingham Junction, and a further ascent, also partly at 1 in 80, between Worstead and North Walsham.

The ENR stations were built as cheaply as possible, their simple timber-framed buildings being, in effect, the Victorian equivalent of "Portakabins". By Victorian standards, such buildings would have seemed hideously-plain, and there were many indications that the Whitlingham to North Walsham line had been rushed into operation before its stations were fully completed.

The Cromer Extension

Facilities for "goods, coal and cattle traffic" were brought into use in March, 1875, and at the half-year ENR meeting held in September 1875 the East Norfolk shareholders were told that total receipts for all traffic "as rendered by the GER for the half year" were £4,220.[11] After deductions had been made, this left a small but encouraging surplus of £1,601; however, warned the Chairman, the long term prosperity of the line "depended very much upon building operations at Cromer". On an optimistic note, the Chairman added that arrangements had been made for "the immediate commencement of . . . works on the Cromer extension", and these works would be carried out under the supervision of Mr J. Cooke, who had "lately constructed the Watton & Swaffham line".[12]

John Cook was a company agent rather than an engineer, and in this context it is interesting to note that the East Norfolk Railway had employed a variety of contractors and engineers before the East Norfolk Directors eventually formed an amicable relationship with Lucas Brothers – a well-known civil engineering firm that had been founded at Lowestoft in 1847. A giant among Victorian contractors, Lucas Brothers was a long-standing partnership between Charles Thomas Lucas (1820–93) and his brother Thomas (later Sir Thomas) Lucas. The firm was, from its inception, associated with the large-scale pre-fabrication of wooden buildings, and it seems likely that the widespread use of timber-framed buildings on the East Norfolk line was a direct result of Lucas Brothers' involvement in the scheme.

While Lucas Brothers carried out the actual work of construction, they did not undertake surveying or other engineering duties, and for that purpose the company employed Edward Wilson & Co. as engineers. Edward Wilson himself is unlikely to have spent much time on a comparatively minor project such as the ENR, and in practice, day-to-day supervision of the works was carried out by his nephew, Mr John Wilson, who lived in North Norfolk while the railway was being built.[13]

Plant from the Watton & Swaffham line was used on the Cromer extension contract (presumably through the agency of John Cook), and it seems that, on average, about 150 navvies were employed on the works.

Completion to Cromer

The extension commenced "in the parish of North Walsham in the county of Norfolk by a junction with the railway authorised by The East Norfolk Railway Act 1864" and terminated "in the parish of Cromer", a distance of 7 miles 74½ chains.[14] The intervening land was sparsely-populated, but it was intended that an intermediate station would be provided to serve Lord Suffield's estate at Gunton Park. Indeed, much of the land required for the new railway belonged to the East Norfolk Chairman, and Lord Suffield was able to furnish plentiful supplies of ballast and brick clay from his own property.

In February 1876, the company announced that work on the extension was in active progress",[15] but the terrain beyond North Walsham was more difficult than that between North Walsham and Whitlingham, and faced with an intervening ridge of higher land the railway builders made relatively slow progress. The works were, nevertheless, in an advanced state by the summer of 1876, and on 29th July, 1876 the line was opened as far as Gunton – from where a service of horse-drawn omnibuses provided a tenuous link to and from Cromer. Finally, on 26th March, 1877, the East Norfolk Railway was completed throughout, and trains commenced running between Norwich and the growing seaside resort of Cromer – a distance of 23 miles and 79 chains.

The completed railway was single track throughout between Whitlingham Junction and Cromer, although, to prevent congestion on the "main line" section between Norwich and Whitlingham, the former Norwich & Yarmouth line had been doubled to accommodate East Norfolk traffic. At Cromer, the branch terminated at some distance from the seashore, on an elevated site beside the Norwich Road. In 1877, however, this inconvenient position was of little consequence, and the railway's supporters were glad that, after so many disappointments, their railway was at last complete.

The branch was, in many ways, an interesting mixture of Great Eastern and non-Great Eastern practice. Its permanent way, for example, was of typical GER pattern, with 80 lb per yard bullhead rail resting in cast iron chairs attached to transverse wooden sleepers; the latter were. by modern standards, widely-spaced, with a gap of 3 ft between each one (except at rail joints, where the sleepers were brought closer together).

Early Train Services

There were originally about half a dozen trains each way between Norwich and Cromer, average times, for the 24 mile journey being around 60 minutes. In 1882, for example, the normal weekday passenger timetable provided 7 up and 7 down services, with departures from Cromer at 6.30, 8.50, 10.10 am, 12.30, 3.30, 6.35 and 8.05 pm. In the reverse direction, balancing down trains left Norwich at 7.25, 9.02, 11.18 am, 1.30, 4.22, 6.47 and 9.02 pm. The 3.30 pm up and 11.18 am down trains were "Parliamentary" workings, while the early morning train from Norwich was a mixed formation conveying both passenger vehicles and goods rolling stock; potential travellers were warned that such trains were "goods trains with passenger carriages attached for the convenience of the public" – and normal punctuality could not always be observed.

London connections were given for both Liverpool Street and St Pancras (via the Tottenham & Hampstead Joint line) but there was no indication which, if any, services conveyed through portions. There were as yet no fast Cromer to London services via the Wensum Curve (which avoided Norwich Thorpe) and the best morning up services offered a journey time from Cromer to Liverpool Street of 4 hours 15 minutes. In the down direction, travellers on the 9.10 am and 5.15 pm departures from Liverpool Street arrived in Cromer at 2.32 pm and 9.57 pm respectively, and with journey times such as these there was little incentive for long-distance commuters to consider Cromer as a possible seaside home.

The End of Local Control

Having originated as an independent company with its own corporate identity the East Norfolk Railway was gradually taken over by Great Eastern interests as that company increased its financial stake in the ENR and took an ever-greater interest in East Norfolk affairs. There was, on the other hand, no obvious moment at which Great Eastern influence became dominant, and indeed, the GER would not have assumed control so rapidly if local investors had shown more interest in the scheme. In a sense, the GER controlled the East Norfolk by default, and this was evident as early as 1872 when it was reported that £29,300 worth of ENR shares were held by the GER, whereas Lord Suffield and other local supporters had subscribed only £24,780.

Finding themselves the holders of over half of the East Norfolk company's subscribed capital, the Great Eastern Directors were able to exercise control over the ENR from an early date, and when Cromer started to provide lucrative passenger traffic for the parent company, it was only a matter of time before the Great Eastern Railway assumed full control of its tiny *protégé*. In the event, the East Norfolk company retained its nominal independence until the 1880s, but, in 1881, the Great Eastern obtained Parliamentary consent for a full amalgamation, and the short life of the East Norfolk Railway Company was brought to an amicable conclusion.

The East Norfolk branch had been worked by the GER from its inception, and as far as everyday operation was concerned the effects of the take-over were minimal; the local Directors probably felt that unwelcome responsibility had been taken out of their hands – while ordinary travellers were probably blissfully unaware that a change of ownership had taken place!

Sources for Chapter One

1 *Bradshaw's Shareholders' Manual*; *The Journal of the House of Commons 1862*.
2 *The Journal of the House of Commons 1864*.
3 *The Journal of the House of Lords 1864*.
4 *The Journal of the House of Commons 1864*.
5 ENR Act 1864 (27 & 28 Vic. cap. 122).
6 ENR Half-yearly report, *The Railway Times*, 24th September, 1864 p. 1284
7 *Ibid.*
8 *Bradshaw's Shareholders' Manual 1864*, p. 78.
9 ENR Half-yearly report, *The Railway Times*.
10 ENR Act 1872 (38 & 39 Vic. cap. 17).
11 ENR Half-yearly report, *The Railway Times*, 11th September, 1875.
12 *Ibid.*
13 R.S. Joby, *The East Norfolk Railway*.
14 ENR Act 1872 (38 & 39 Vic. cap. 17).
15 ENR Half-yearly report, *The Railway Times*.

EAST NORFOLK RAILWAY.

DOWN TRAINS.

Miles from Norwich	From		Week Days Mxd. morn	morn	Parl. morn	morn	morn	morn		morn	Mrkt even.	Mxd. Mrkt even.	even.	even.	even.	even.	even.		Sundays even.	Pri. even.		
	LONDON L'pool St.	dep.	—	5 10	6 0	7 35	9 10	9 0	...	11 55	Saturdays only.	Saturdays only.	2 30	2 40	...	5 0	5 15	—	—	2 40	—	—
	LONDON St. Pancras	„	—	—	—	7 33	9 15	...	...	12 3			—	2 36	—	—	5 5	—	—	...	—	—
	Cambridge	„	—	—	8 36	10 8	10 45	...	...	1 38			—	4 17	—	—	6 40	—	—	4 [illegible]	—	—
	Ely	„	—	—	8 57	11 13		—	...	2 5			—	4 45	—	—	7 5	—	—	5 30	—	—
	Lynn	„	—	—	8 52	—		—	...	12 32			—	3 12	4 40	—	5 40	—	—	—	—	—
	Dereham	„	—	7 22	10 2	10 59		—	—	1 48			...	4 20	5 40	—	6 56	—	—	—	—	—
	Ipswich	„	...	7 8	-	—		11 20	...	...			4 35	...	...	6 45	—	—	—	—	—	...
	Yarmouth (V.)	dep.	6 10	8 10	10 20	—		...	...	3 45	3 45	...	5 35			...		—	1 5	—	—	—
	Lowestoft	„	...	7†12	10 5	—		...	—	3 30	3 10	...	5 18			...		—	12 47	...	—	—
—	Norwich (T)	dep.	7 25	9 2	11 18	1 30			...	4 22	4 35	5 20		6 47		9 2		—	[illegible]	8 46	—	—
2	Whitlingham	„	7 31	9 8	11 24	1 38			—	4 28	4 41	5 26		6 52		9 8		—	2 16	8 51	—	—
6	Salhouse	„	7 40	...	11 32	1 46			—	4 37	4 50	5 37		7 2		9 17		—	2 25	9 0	—	—
8¾	Wroxham	„	7 47	9 23	11 41	1 55			...	4 45	4 57	5 46		7 10		9 24		—	2 32	9 7	—	—
—	Wroxham	dep.	7 50	9 25	11 45	1 58			L	4 47	4 59	5 50		7 12		9 27		...	...	...	—	...
11¼	Coltishall	„	7 56	9 31	11 51	2 4			L	4 53	5 5	5 56		7 18		9 33		...	...	...	—	—
14¼	Buxton Lamas	„	8 2	9 37	11 57	2 10			L	4 59	5 11	6 2		7 24		9 39		...	...	—	—	—
17½	Aylsham	„	8 10	9 45	12 5	2 14			L	5 8	5 20	6 11		7 33		9 48		...	...	—	—	—
22	Cawston	„	8 19	9 54	12 14	2 27			L	5 17	5 29	6 20		7 42		9 57		...	—	—	—	—
24	Reepham	„	8 24	9 59	12 19	2 32			L	5 22	5 34	6 25		7 47		10 2		...	—	...	...	...
13¼	Worstead	dep.	7 57	...	11 50	2 5			...	4 53	...	5 58		7 19		9 33		—	2 41	9 16	—	—
16	Nth Walsham	„	8 5	9 37	11 57	2 14			...	5 0	...	6 8		7 28		9 40		...	2 48	9 24	—	—
19½	Gunton	„	8 15	9 45	12 5	2 23			—	5 8	...	6 18		7 37		9 48		—	2 56	9 31	—	—
24	CROMER		8 25	9 53	12 15	2 32			...	5 17	...	6 28		7 45		9 57		...	3 5	9 40	—	—

UP TRAINS.

Miles from Cromer	From		Week Days morn		morn	morn	even.	Mrkt even.	N even.		even.	Mxd. even.	even.					Sundays Parl. even.	even.			
	CROMER	dep.	6 30		8 50	10 10	12 30	N	3 30		6 33	7 0	8 5	...	...	...	...	12 50	7 30	—	—	—
4¼	Gunton	„	6 39		8 59	10 19	12 39	...	3 39		6 42	7 11	8 14	—	—	...	—	12 59	7 39	—	—	—
8	Nth Walsham	„	6 47		9 8	10 27	12 50	...	3 48		6 51	7 30	8 23	—	...	...	...	1 8	7 48	...	—	—
10½	Worstead	„	6 53		9 14	10 33	12 57	...	3 54		6 57	7 38	8 29	...	...	...	...	1 14	7 54	—	—	—
	Reepham	dep.	6 23		8 40	10 5	12 28	3 20	3 25		6 29	...	8 0	...	—	—	...	—	—	—	—	—
	Cawston	„	6 28		8 45	10 10	12 33	3 25	3 30		6 34	...	8 5		—	—	...	...	...	—	...	...
	Aylsham	„	6 37		8 54	10 19	12 42	3 34	L. 3 39		6 43	...	8 14	...	—	—	—	—	—	—	...	...
	Buxton Lamas	„	6 45		9 2	10 27	12 50	3 42	3 47		6 51	...	8 22	...	—	—	—	...	...	—	...	...
	Coltishall	„	6 51		9 8	10 33	12 56	3 48	3 53		6 57	...	8 28	—	—	...	—	...	...	—	...	—
	Wroxham	arr.	6 57		9 14	10 39	1 2	3 54	3 59		7 3	...	8 34	...	—	...	—	...	...	—	...	—
13½	Wroxham	dep.	7 2		9 29	10 44	1 8	3 55	4 6		7 10	7 50	8 39	...	—	...	—	1 24	8 4	...	...	—
18	Salhouse	„	•		9 35	10 50	1 15	...	4 11		7 16	•	8 46	—	—	...	—	1 30	8 10	...	...	—
22	Whitlingham	„	7 15		9 45	11 1	1 26	4 8	4 21		7 26	8 7	8 55	...	—	...	...	1 39	8 20	—	...	—
24	Norwich (T)	arr.	7 20		9 50	11 7	1 32	4 13	4 28		7 32	8 15	9 0	...		...	...	1 45	8 28	...	...	...
	Lowestoft	arr.	8 42		M	12 15	2 30	5 7	6 37		...	...	9 57	—	—	...	—	3 8	9 50	—	—	—
	Yarmouth (V)	„	8 45		10 53	11 57	2 12	4 50	6 20		...	...	9 40		..	...	—	2 32	9 [illegible]	—	—	—
	Ipswich	arr.	9 0	—	11 55		...	Saturdays only.	6 25	..	...	Saturdays only.	—	...	—	...	—	—	—	—	—	—
	Dereham	„	Mndys. only.	9 31	11§20	1 37	4 8		—	O 54	8 57		—	—	—	...	—	—	—	—	—	—
	Lynn	„		10 23	12§0	2 50	5 17		...	8 0			...	—	—	...	—	—	—	—	—	—
	Ely	„		9 7	—	12 50	4 6		—	8 28	—		12 10	—	—	...	—	8 [illegible]	12 [illegible]	—	—	—
	Cambridge	„		9 36	—	1 20	4 35		...	8 55	—		12 56	—	...	—	—	8 57	12 37	—	—	—
	LONDON. St. Pancras	„		11 14	—	3 [illegible]	6 12		...	8 55	—		—	—	...	—	—	—	—	—	—	—
	LONDON. L'pool St.	„	10 45	11 10	2 10	2 52	6 8		8 15	8 30	—		3 30	...	...	—	—	7 0	3 30	—	—	—

☞ Horses and Private Carriages not conveyed by these Trains.
• Will call only when required to take up or set down Passengers.
L Not between Wroxham and Reepham on Saturdays.
N Parly from East Norfolk Line Stations.
§ Due at Dereham at 11.3 a.m., and runs to Lynn on Tuesdays only
‡ Mondays only. † From Lowestoft at 7.35 a.m. on Mondays.
M To Yarmouth on Wednesdays only.
O Due at Dereham at 5.40 p.m. on Saturdays.

The 1882 Passenger Timetable for the East Norfolk Railway.

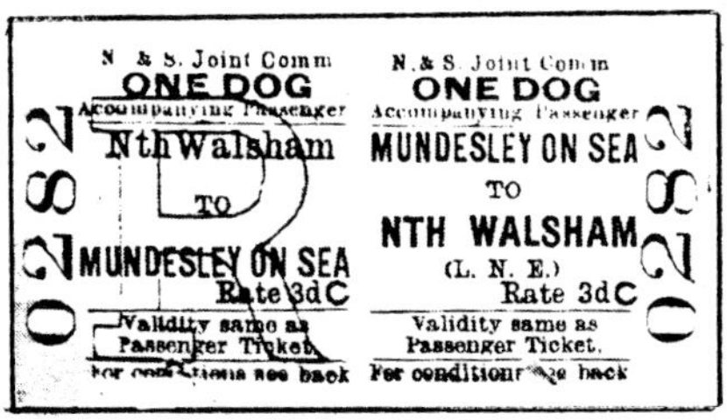

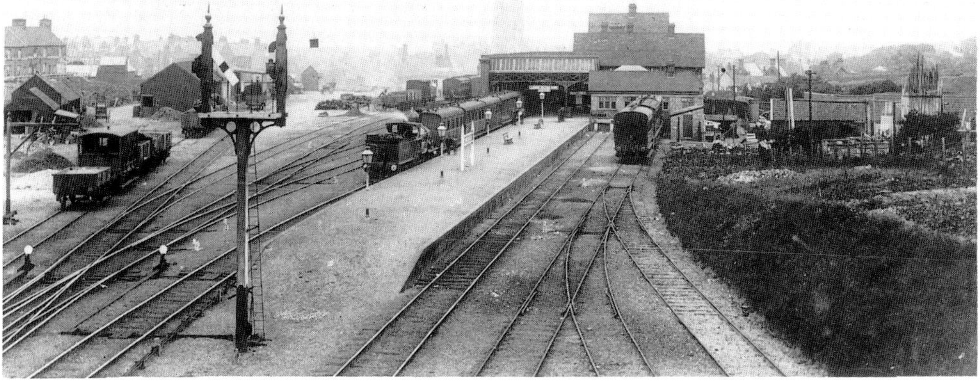

A panoramic view of Cromer Beach – probably photographed around 1890 from the original signal cabin; an M & GN; 4–4–0 pauses in the main platform with a train of short-wheelbase stock. *Lens of Sutton*

Cromer High in the early years of the Century with an 0–4–4T standing in the bay platform. *J. Kite*

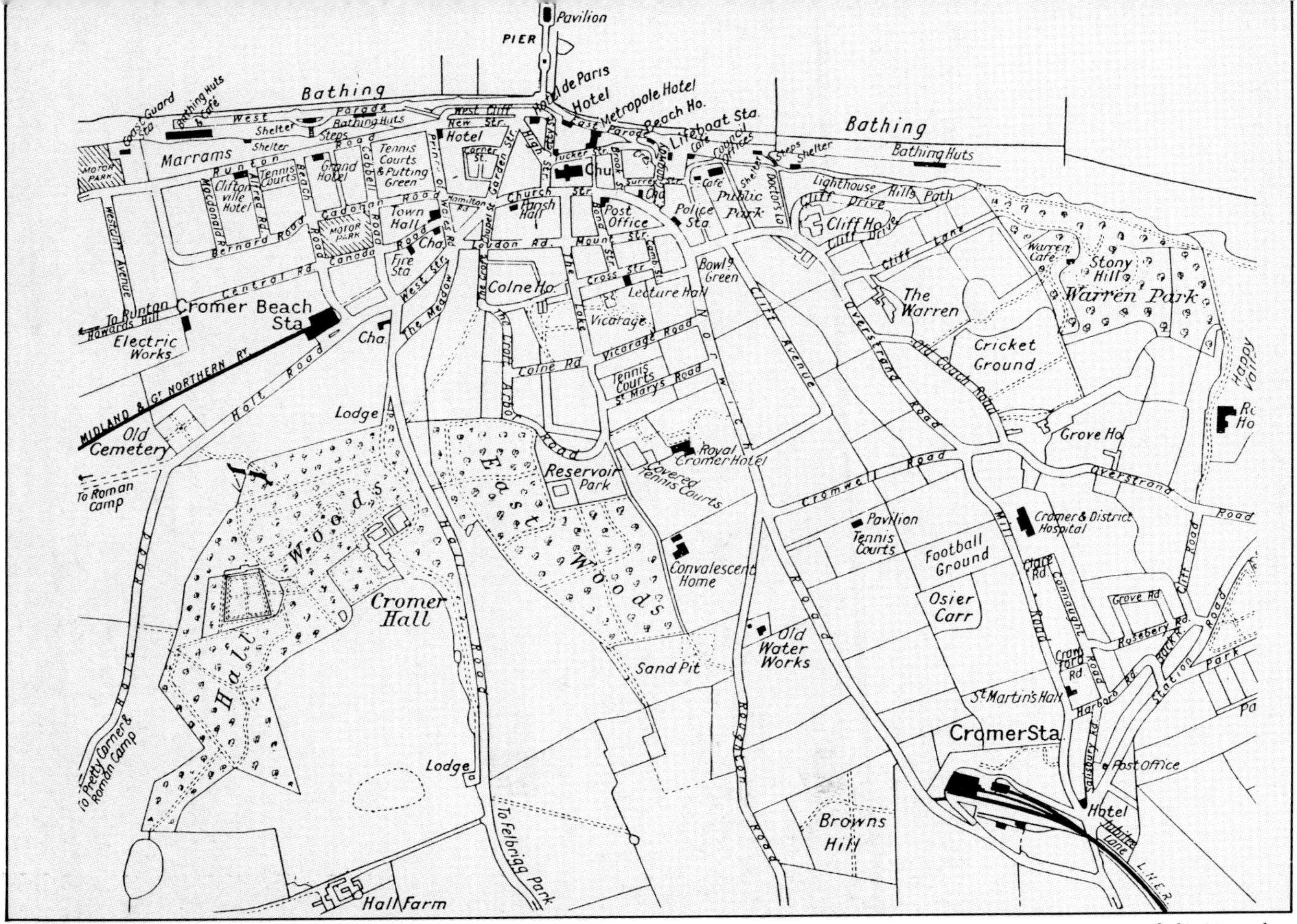

Street plan of Cromer around 1930, showing the position of the GER station (*bottom right*) and the M & GN terminus (*top left*). Note that "Station Road" leads to the (*earlier*) Great Eastern station.
Courtesy Ward Lock & Co., Red Guide

A beautiful photograph of Cromer Beach station with an immaculate Midland locomotive, crew and staff posing for the camera, *c.*1903 (see *page 34*).

Oakwood Collection

Chapter Two

Expansion of the System (1882–1906)

The opening of the East Norfolk Railway effectively transformed Cromer from a quaint fishing settlement into a fashionable seaside resort, and in the next few years this hitherto remote and isolated little town grew rapidly as new hotels, villas and guest houses mushroomed along the clifftops to the east and west of the original town centre. Some of these new hotels were large, prestigious establishments that would not have been out-of-place in London, Paris or other major cities, and the appearance of such large and impressive structures was visible proof of Cromer's success as a middle class Victorian seaside town.

Writing in the June 1898 *Railway Magazine*, Mr V.L. Whitechurch clearly remembered Cromer's period of 19th century growth, and it would be of interest to quote in some detail from this valuable eye-witness account:

> It was back in the summer of far back 1877 when first I visited Cromer . . . the railway had only been opened to Cromer during the previous March, and it was still a little village – very beautiful, but very quiet. The railway was not then the property of the Great Eastern; although worked by that company it was owned by the East Norfolk Railway Company.
>
> Not until 1881 did the Great Eastern become the actual proprietors of the line, but . . . they controlled the destinies of Cromer . . . and to that most enterprising company Cromer owes, in the first instance, its present prosperity. Of course its great natural beauty, its picturesque position, its health-giving and invigorating air, all entitle it to the honourable place amongst seaside resorts that it has attained; but great as are its natural advantages it would still probably "blush unseen and waste its sweetness on the desert air" but for the aid and encouragement given to it by the Great Eastern . . . But all the outside help in the world would never have made Cromer the thriving resort it is had not its inhabitants risen to the occasion. That they have done so, the rows of pretty but substantially built villas amply testify. Comfortable and admirably conducted boarding-houses, too, abound on all sides.
>
> The principal hotel at Cromer is, of course, the Grand. This truly magnificent building faces full upon the sea, and is, perhaps, from an architectural point of view, the most imposing edifice in the town. Built in 1891, it possesses all the most modern conveniences. Its three principal corridors are 170 feet in length, and it has accommodation for 150 people. It stands on the west cliff, with a broad expanse of green between it and the cliff's edge. The views from its windows are charming, both seaward and also inland over the wooded hills. Second in importance to the Grand is the Hôtel Métropole, situated in the centre of the town, close by the old parish church, but also overlooking the sea. Erected in 1894, it is, like the Grand, thoroughly up to date in all appointments, yet withal most cosy and comfortable, with some charming views of the coast and cliffs from the eastwards side. The catering at either hotel is all that could be desired, and as both have been fitted throughout by Messrs Trevor, Page & Co., of Norwich, it is needless to say that the furnishing, from an artistic point of view, cannot be surpassed."

Victorian visitors, arriving in Cromer for the first time, would obviously have been impressed by the massive new hotels, but hotel development was just one example of the way that the resort was transformed by the opening of the railway. Sea walls, for example, were built to protect the town's spectacular, but friable cliffs, and these new coast defences provided a

An interesting early view of Wroxham station, showing the rear of the original East Norfolk wooden station building and the first signalbox; both of these buildings had disappeared by the end of the 19th Century. *Lens of Sutton*

On 3rd November, 1895 the GER ran an experimental non-stop train between Liverpool Street and Cromer. Holden oil-fired 2–2–2 No. 1006 and its 8-coach train (consisting of 6-short wheelbase vehicles and 2 bogie coaches) travelled via Ipswich and Wensum Curve (Norwich), reaching Cromer on one 3,100 gallon tenderful of water; here the special is seen speeding through Worstead with station master Frederick Avery on the extreme right. *Lens of Sutton*

variety of attractive walks and promenades. Nearby, on breezy cliffs beyond the lighthouse, the 18-hole Royal Cromer Golf Club was established in 1887 to cater for the resort's upper middle class patrons. A further attraction for summer visitors was the pier, which extended seawards for 183 yds and replaced the town's ancient wooden jetty; the pier was completed in 1899 at a cost of £11,000.[16]

The Origins of "Poppyland"

It is interesting to find that much of Cromer's Victorian popularity stemmed from an accidental discovery of the area by newspaper correspondent Clement Scott (1841–1904), who, tired of more sophisticated British or European resorts, had written enthusiastically of what he called "a queer, ancient, rambling village". Scott's now-forgotten poem *The Garden of Sleep*, and his evocation of "Poppyland" made Cromer into a mecca for contemporary writers and *littérateurs*, and the soubriquet "Poppyland" survived for many years as an important element in local tourist publicity.

Contemporary writers well-understood the part played by Clement Scott in the popularisation of Cromer, and V.L. Whitechurch in the aforementioned article recalled that it was "somewhere about the year 1888" that Mr Scott composed *The Garden of Sleep*. Mr Isodore de Lara then set the words to music, and the resulting ballad rapidly became one of the most popular songs in circulation:

> Soulful tenors told how "On the grass of the cliff at the edge of the steep, God planted a garden – the garden of sleep!" Young ladies warbled sweetly of "Brief days of desire and long dreams of delight," and all the world knew that a "tower in ruins stands guard o'er the deep" at a little spot called Overstrand, situated close by Cromer.

Amusingly, *The Garden of Sleep* provoked considerable criticism in certain literary and theatrical circles, and one gentleman suggested that Scott's whimsical verses were "the dream of an opium eater". V.L. Whitechurch hinted (probably correctly) that such criticism was merely retaliation from writers who had themselves been savaged in Mr Scott's *Daily Telegraph* theatre column – but whatever the literary merits of *The Garden of Sleep* the fact remains that it was instrumental in placing "Poppyland" on the Victorian tourist's map.

Rival Schemes

The exploitation of "Poppyland" was welcomed by the GER, but the company was not able to secure a monopoly of Cromer traffic, and on 16th June, 1887 the Eastern & Midlands Railway opened a rival station on a prime site to the north west of the Great Eastern terminus. The Eastern & Midlands was a lineal descendent of earlier, "Railway Mania" schemes that had hoped to build competitive east-to-west cross country lines across Norfolk in opposition to the ECR. Its history is complex, but briefly the E&M originated in the 1860s when the Midlands & Eastern Railway had amalgamated with two smaller railways, thereby bringing a 36½ mile branch from the Great

Northern at Bourne under unified management. By this means, the GNR was able to reach Kings Lynn in opposition to the rival Great Eastern Railway. Meanwhile, the opening of a Midland-backed line from Peterborough to Sutton Bridge on 1st August, 1866 had brought another company into the arena.

Eastwards, other interests were actively promoting a somewhat tenuous chain of local railways, and when these lines were opened (at various times between 1877 and 1883) they effectively carried the Midlands & Eastern route from Lynn to Great Yarmouth. On 18th August, 1882 the lines east of Lynn were amalgamated as the Eastern & Midlands Railway, and a year later the Eastern & Midlands absorbed the earlier Midlands & Eastern and Peterborough to Sutton Bridge lines. The result of these complicated amalgamations was a lengthy "main line" from the GNR at Bourne, extending east to Great Yarmouth, with branches from Sutton Bridge to Peterborough and from Melton Constable to Norwich.

Curiously, the Eastern & Midlands reached Cromer more or less by accident, and in order to understand how and why this alternative route to Cromer was built, it is necessary to say a little more about the pre-history of the Eastern & Midlands company. One must, in particular look more closely at the Lynn & Fakenham Railway, which, on 13th July, 1876, had obtained an Act for construction of a railway running eastwards from Gaywood Junction, on the Lynn & Hunstanton branch, to Fakenham, a distance of 18¾ miles. Supporters of the Lynn & Fakenham included Lord Townsend (a major Norfolk landowner), Sir W.A. Browne-Folkes, and the Rev I.L. Brereton,[17] and as far as can be ascertained none of these gentlemen were in any way connected with the East Norfolk or with any other GER-backed lines.

The Lynn & Fakenham Bill had been opposed by the Great Eastern which was understandably wary of any incursion into its East Anglian heartlands. The GER was especially concerned at the threat of any northwards or westwards continuation of the Lynn & Fakenham beyond its existing terminus, and these fears were realised when, in 1880, the Fakenham company obtained Parliamentary consent for extensions from Melton Constable to Norwich and Blakeney.

The Lynn & Fakenham was opened throughout to Norwich on 2nd December, 1882, but the Blakeney line was not proceeded with. Noting the success of Cromer, Hunstanton, and other railway-linked resorts, the Lynn & Fakenham Railway was nevertheless keen to extend its own line northwards to the coast, and the L&F company made several attempts to reach Blakeney or some other point on the north Norfolk coast. On 11th August, 1882, for instance, the Lynn & Fakenham Directors obtained further powers for an extension from Blakeney to the neighbouring village of Stiffkey, and, although this project never materialised, the Blakeney scheme was eventually amended to serve the more promising resorts of Cromer and Sheringham. In the meantime, the Lynn & Fakenham had been amalgamated with the Yarmouth & North Norfolk and Yarmouth Union Railways to form the Eastern & Midlands, the necessary Act being obtained in 1882.[18]

As we have seen, the Eastern & Midlands line to Cromer was opened on 16th June, 1887 – by which time the E&M main line was functioning as a west-to-east cross country route in opposition to the Great Eastern Railway. In 1893, the Eastern & Midlands Railway was taken over by the parent Midland and Great Northern companies, and a new organisation – the Midland & Great Northern Joint railway – was created to administer the former E&M system.

Further Extensions

The Great Eastern initially regarded the Midland & Great Northern and its progenitors as intruders in Norfolk, and in response to this attack on GER territory, the company persuaded its ally the East Norfolk Railway to build a branch running westwards from Wroxham to a junction with the GER Wells–Dereham branch at County School. This 23 mile 51 chain cross country line was a classic "political" route; running through sparsely-populated countryside that can have contributed little originating traffic, it was opened in several stages, reaching Buxton Lamas on 8th July, 1879, and Aylsham on 1st January, 1880.

Although the East Norfolk Railway was still nominally-independent, this new line was clearly the Great Eastern's counter-attack in the face of Lynn & Fakenham aggression, and while the latter was itself being built in stages just a few miles to the north, the GER line was slowly pushed westwards to reach Cawston on 1st September, 1880 and Reepham by 2nd May, 1881.[19] Finally, on 1st May, 1882 the line was completed throughout to its junction with the Wells branch; there was no station at the point of convergence, the "junction" of the two lines being at County School – a new station that had been opened to serve the nearby 'Norfolk County School'.

Completion of the System

The Midland & Great Northern touched the GER at Cromer, Aylsham and at North Walsham – where the M&GN passed beneath the East Norfolk route before turning south to run beside its rival for about 1 mile. Although the two organisations had initially viewed each other with suspicion, the M&GN and Great Eastern soon saw the advantages of co-operation, and in 1896 they obtained an Act for a jointly owned branch running north eastwards from North Walsham to the seaside village of Mundesley.

The Mundesley scheme had originated in 1888 as a purely Eastern & Midlands venture which (if completed as planned) would have provided a short branch running from North Walsham to Mundesley-on-Sea, but the scheme was subsequently amended to permit joint ownership of a longer line running through the heart of Clement Scott's famed "Poppyland". It was proposed that the original line from Mundesley would be continued along the coast, through Overstrand, to Cromer, at which place a system of junctions would allow trains to use either the GER or M&GN stations.

In theory, any railway through the "Poppyland" area should have been an immense success. Mundesley and Overstrand were both highly-picturesque

An early view of West Runton station with its simple style building. *J. Kite*

Mundesley station shortly after its opening. Like all of the original Norfolk & Suffolk Joint line stations, Mundesley was lavishly equipped in expectation of a busy holiday traffic in years to come. *Lens of Sutton*

villages, and quite apart from their well publicised associations with the "Garden of Sleep" at nearby Sidestrand, these coastal villages had already gained popularity with small numbers of regular visitors who were able to reach their holiday homes by "a well-appointed pair-horse omnibus plying between North Walsham and the Ship and Royal Hotels, Mundesley".[20] There were however, suspicions that the projected railway through "Poppy-land" would *not* be welcomed by those who had already discovered the area and wished to keep it unspoiled by the more blatant forms of commercial exploitation.

The new line was built in two stages, and the lower section, from North Walsham to Mundesley was ready for opening by the summer of 1898. In June, *The Railway Magazine* reported that the line was "rapidly approaching completion" and when opened, it would "bring Mundesley, a most picturesque little seaside resort, within three hours journey of London". The railway was opened for goods traffic on 1st June, 1898, and for passengers just one month later on 1st July.

The new branch was connected to both the GER and M&GN stations at North Walsham, the distance from North Walsham Town (M&GN) being 5 miles 3 chains. An intermediate station was provided at Paston & Knapton, and train services were provided by the Great Eastern and Midland & Great Northern companies. For administrative and operational purposes the line was vested in a newly-created organisation known as "The Norfolk & Suffolk Joint Committee" – a committee of four Great Eastern, two Great Northern and two Midland Directors (this committee also administered the jointly-owned Yarmouth to Lowestoft line).

The Mundesley branch ran at a loss for several months, but in the summer of 1899 a modest profit of £200 was recorded, and this small operating surplus must have encouraged the Joint Committee to start work on the northern continuation from Mundesley to Cromer. Land purchases were complete by 1902, and construction work commenced in the early part of the following year. A few months later, in September 1904, it was reported that the earthworks from Mundesley to Cromer were "well-advanced",[21] though the junctions at Cromer had "not yet been commenced".

Although construction entailed many large earthworks, the sandy soil encountered *en route* to Cromer should have presented few problems, and well-informed commentators wondered if the long-delayed completion to Cromer was evidence of some ulterior motive on the part of the Great Eastern, Midland and Great Northern companies.

G.A. Sekon was convinced that the Mundesley to Cromer line was an entirely "political" route concocted by the three owning companies in an effort to avoid undue competition, and in September 1904 he openly accused the three companies of duplicity:

> The railways concerned do not even pretend that the new railway can ever pay. The few hundreds of passengers that will be carried during the short summer season to the villages of Overstrand, Sidestrand, and Trimingham is, with the small local traffic, all that the line between Cromer and Mundesley can obtain, whilst the portion between Cromer and Runton is solely to give the Great Eastern

> Railway an entrance to Sheringham . . . Doubtless the desire of the competing lines to keep each other out of the district was the cause of the Cromer–Mundesley line being projected . . .[22]

If the GER and M&GN were genuinely interested in the provision of improved railway facilities, argued Sekon, they would have collaborated in the planning and construction of "a central and commodious joint station in Cromer". This central station could have been served by a much shorter and more direct connecting line than the one actually proposed, and moreover, such a line "connecting the two existing stations . . . could have been constructed without taking any extra property within the town, as it could have been laid out at the rear of existing buildings". As it was, claimed Sekon, "the opportunity was not taken" and the projected line would avoid Cromer completely, adding "about 3 miles to the . . . mileage of each train".

Although these arguments may have been over-stated, the fact remains that the 8 mile, coastal line between Mundesley and Cromer took a suspiciously long time to complete, and it is possible that some of G.A. Sekon's fears were justified. There is some evidence that responsible railway officers such as the GER Engineer and the Midland General Manager had privately criticised the entire scheme – the latter is said to have asked "where all the money was coming from" to pay for the line, while John Wilson, the Great Eastern Engineer, felt that goods sheds would be an unnecessary luxury. At the same time, local landowners were antipathetic and un-cooperative, and William Marriott, the M&GN Engineer, recalled that the railway-builders were "badly hit by the high prices" asked for land.[23]

Some blame for the delays has also been attributed to Robert Finnegan, who had been awarded a contract for construction of the line from Mundesley to Cromer. Mr Finnegan was said to have been an "unmethodical" worker, and in an attempt to instill more discipline into his work, the Joint Committee asked him to report every incident, large or small. Amusingly, the contractor was not the reporting type, and when his 0–4–0 tank locomotive repeatedly derailed itself on the temporary way, he is said to have telegraphed the following message to his employers:

ON AGAIN – OFF AGAIN – ON AGAIN – FINNEGAN!

(Sadly, this tale appears to be pure fabrication, and it is worth noting that an identical message is supposed to have been sent by a Tasmanian station master called Lonnegan).

Eventually, on 23rd July, 1906, the coastal line was completed throughout from Mundesley to Cromer. Approaching Cromer from the east, the new line tunnelled beneath the Great Eastern station to reach its junction with the GER at Roughton Road. Westwards, the line continued to a triangular junction with the M&GN which facilitated through running to Sheringham (via Newstead Lane Junction and Runton West Junction) or into the M&GN station at Cromer Beach (via Newstead Land and Runton East Junction).

The completed line enabled GER trains to reach Sheringham, while at the same time the M&GN was provided with an alternative, albeit much longer path for trains running between North Walsham and Melton Constable. The Norfolk & Suffolk Joint had lavish intermediate stations, designed to accommodate the holiday traffic that was expected to materialise. Mundesley and Paston stations had been built by Messrs Cornish & Gaymer, while Overstrand and Trimingham were erected by C.A. Sadler of Sheringham; Mundesley was said to have been "one of the prettiest and best . . . for many miles around".[24] The principal engineering feature on the new railway was a five span viaduct carrying the line across Runton Common between Newstead Lane and Runton West junctions.

From its inception, the Norfolk and Suffolk Joint route was worked by trains of both owning companies, the usual practice being for Great Eastern branch trains to use the GER station at North Walsham, while their M&GN counterparts ran to and from the nearby Midland & Great Northern station.

The M&GN provided a handful of through services from Cromer Beach to North Walsham and return, and there were several short-distance M&GN workings between Cromer and Overstrand or between North Walsham and Mundesley. The Great Eastern, meanwhile, offered a limited service of local trains from North Walsham to Overstrand – from where fans of Clement Scott could walk along breezy clifftops to see the "Garden of Sleep" at Sidestrand churchyard. In addition to these modest branch services, the GER added through Mundesley and Sheringham portions to its principal London expresses (these will be considered in greater detail in the following chapter).

19th Century Motive Power

Although Victorians were obsessively interested in all aspects of technology, they do not seem to have been interested in "train spotting", and indeed the idea of spending hour after hour passively recording engine numbers would have been regarded as a completely useless pastime! It follows that we do not have detailed descriptions of day-to-day operations on rural branch lines such as the Cromer route, and one can only speculate as to the types of locomotives seen at Cromer in the first few years.

The famous 'Y' class 2–4–0s were a long-lived and widely-used class, and it seems reasonable to suggest that these engines were used on the Cromer branch at, or shortly after, the time of its opening.

Designed by Robert Sinclair, the 'Y' class was built by various engineering firms between 1859 and 1866, and although intended for freight duties they were also used for passenger work. The 'Y' class had 17 in. x 24 in. outside cylinders, and 6 ft 1 in. coupled wheels; their weight, in full working order, was about 54 tons. The engines were numbered in sequence from 307 to 416, and the class totalled no less than 110 machines. In later years, most of these locomotives were rebuilt and modernised, and two of the rebuilds – Nos. 315 and 316 were stationed at Cromer in the 1880s. Another engine likely to have been used on the East Norfolk line was No. 328, which was based at Norwich for several years.[25]

The 'Y' class was withdrawn over a twelve year period between 1882 and 1894, one of the last to be scrapped being No. 0308 (ex 308) which was thirty five years old at the time of its demise.

Many of the duties previously undertaken by the 'Y' class were later worked by Johnson's "No. 1 Class" 2–4–0s, which, like their slightly earlier predecessors, were widely used throughout East Anglia. Originally built for service on the North British Railway, the first "No. 1 Class" engines were delivered to the GER in 1867. The initial batch had 6 ft driving wheels and 16 in. x 22 in. cylinders.[26] The engines weighed 47 tons and had a boiler pressure of 140 lb. per square inch. Intended for mixed traffic work, the "No. 1 Class" (or "Little Sharpie") 2–4–0s eventually totalled 45 engines (including the 5 built for NBR service).

In later years, the remaining "No. 1 Class" engines carried Holden boilers, with stove pipe chimneys and domes placed well forward on the front boiler ring; in this form they were attractive little engines, which looked very smart in the Great Eastern's famous dark blue livery. Engines likely to have worked on the Cromer line include Nos. 6, 26, 31, 33, 34 and 49, all of which were stationed at Norwich.[27]

In August 1881 the then locomotive superintendent, Mr Massey Bromley, resigned from office, and he was eventually succeeded by T.W. Worsdell (who was later to become more famous as the NER locomotive chief). One of Worsdell's Great Eastern designs was the 'G14' class – a series of main line 2–4–0s with 7 ft coupled wheels and 18 in. x 24 in. cylinders. Numbered in series from 562 to 571, and from 640 to 649, the 'G14s' sported Worsdell's distinctive "double" splashers, together with Adams-type stovepipe chimneys and cabs of distinctly "Great Western" appearance. The 'G14s' were not entirely successful in main line service, and by the 1890s they had been relegated to branch line duties, in which capacity they regularly worked on the Cromer line; No. 0642 (ex 642) was stationed at Cromer, while Nos. 644–649 were based at Norwich.[28]

It is often forgotten that the Great Eastern once had large numbers of 0–4–4Ts including Bromley's 'E10' class, of which sixty were built between 1878 and 1883; these engines appeared on local services such as those between North Walsham and Mundesley-on-Sea, and also on the main line to Cromer. On 10th September, 1881 one of the 0–4–4Ts was involved in an accident while running bunker first with a heavy excursion. The accident occurred at Cromer, and was later blamed on "insufficient brake power" (see *page 35*).[29]

Some of the engines used on the branch were sub-shedded at Cromer in a single road shed beside the passenger station; the allocation was no more than two engines in the 1880s, but this modest complement could be swelled by incoming excursion or express locomotives that spent the night at Cromer prior to returning to their own depots on the following day.

The opening of the Mundesley branch in June 1898 brought M&GN locomotives onto the Cromer branch in regular service for the first time, while in 1906, the completion of the Mundesley to Cromer line paved the way for an even greater integration of services on the Norfolk & Suffolk Joint line. When first opened, the M&GN local services were worked by Hudswell Clarke 4–4–0Ts formerly owned by the Yarmouth & North Norfolk or Lynn & Fakenham railways, but in 1906 four of these diminutive locomotives were loaned to the Midland Railway, and in their place the MR transferred three 0–4–4Ts to the M&GN. The engines involved were Nos. 142, 143 and 144, and it is interesting to note that, when they came to Norfolk they still carried MR livery; on 23rd July, 1906 No. 143 worked the first Midland & Great Northern train from Mundesley to Cromer Beach.[30]

The Cromer Train Crash

Like most country branches, the Cromer line served the public, in perfect safety, for over a century. In these circumstances, accidents, when they occur, make headline news; furthermore, Board of Trade accident reports often contain many interesting insights into contemporary operating practices, and for this reason it would be useful to examine the 1881 mishap in greater detail.

The train involved in this incident was a 13-coach special, consisting of 11 passenger vehicles and two brake vans. Interestingly, the train had left Cromer as an empty stock working in order to meet a special from Great Yarmouth at North Walsham, and when the excursionists had transferred into the GER special, it departed from North Walsham at 12.17 pm. There were "about 420" passengers aboard, and this heavy formation was travelling at no more than walking speed when it entered Cromer station. The station was, at that time, still a two-platform terminus, and as the main platform was occupied by the 12.30 pm up service to Norwich, the special was signalled into the adjacent bay. Unfortunately, the heavily-loaded excursion could not be brought to a stand, and it ran into some stationary coaches that had been parked at the end of the bay platform.

Although the ensuing collision was not, by any means, a major disaster, it was thoroughly investigated by Major Hutchinson of the Board of Trade, and on 31st August, 1881 the Major reported as follows:

Sir,

I have the honour to report, for the information of the Board of Trade, in compliance with the instructions contained in your minute of the 16th instant, the result of my inquiry into the circumstances connected with the collision which took place on the 11th instant, at Cromer station, on the Great Eastern Railway.

In this case the 12.17 pm down special excursion train from North Walsham entered Cromer station at too high a speed, and came into collision with two empty carriages which were standing at the end of the dock line into which the excursion train had been turned.

Twenty-seven passengers are returned as having been injured.

In the excursion train, which consisted of an 8-wheeled trailing-bogie tank engine running bogie first (weighing about 38½ tons in its condition at the time). and 13 vehicles, of which the front and rear were brake vans, with a guard only in the rear one, supplied with the ordinary hand-brake, two vehicles were slightly damaged, as were also the two empty carriages. The empty carriage next the buffer-stops was forced over them on to the platform, and knocked down a small wooden shed used by the porters.

Cromer station is approached from the south on a rising gradient of 1 in 140, which terminates nearly one mile from the station; there is then a level space for about half a mile, next a falling gradient of 1 in 100 for about 24 chains, and, finally, a still falling gradient of 1 in 300 for about 10 chains. The signal arrangements are of a satisfactory nature, the down home signals being 280 yards south of the buffer stops at the end of the dock line, and 55 yards further from the main line

> buffer stops, with a down distant signal about 800 yards from the down home signals. The signal cabin is about half way between the down home signals and the dock line buffer stops. The line (which is single) is worked with train staff and ticket, and also on the absolute block system; Gunton, 4½ miles from Cromer, and North Walsham, 3½ miles from Gunton, being the two block stations next to Cromer.

Having described the scene of the accident, Major Hutchinson's report then summarised the evidence taken from people who had witnessed the crash. John Bishop, a signalman with five years experience (4½ of them at Cromer) said that he saw the train entering the station at a speed of "about 6 miles an hour". He heard no whistling from the engine, and only when the train had passed Cromer signal box did he think that the speed was "too high for it to stop".

The next witness was station master Francis Benns, who had been in charge of Cromer station since 1877; Mr Benns had been standing near the end of the dock when the train was entering his station:

> When the engine was within about two carriage lengths of the empty carriages, I saw its speed was too high for it to stop clear of the empty carriages. I had time to do nothing, and could not see what the driver was about. I should say the speed on collision with the carriages was 3 or 4 miles an hour. One of the empty carriages was forced over the buffer stops on to the platform level, and knocked down part of a wooden shed forming the porters' room, and then stopped. No wheels were off the rails in the train. I believe the empty carriages were close against the stops, and coupled together. The rails were greasy from a drizzling rain which was falling. I at once went to get the staff from the driver, and despatched the 12.30 up train, which had been detained for six or seven minutes. About half-an-hour afterwards I had a conversation with the driver, and he said it was owing to the rails being greasy that he could not stop. He said the wheels had picked up about the signal cabin, and that afterwards he tried to brake again, but could not stop. He did not mention anything about the guard's brake. I did not hear any brake whistle, which I think I should have done had it been given. The driver was, I think, perfectly sober. I know him well; he has been running in and out of Cromer frequently for the past 18 months, and has never made any mistake previously. The guard told me he had had his brake on tight. I believe he was in the rear van. The usual place for shutting off steam is about the distant signal. The special train had been made up at Cromer and consisted of 11 carriages and two brake vans. The rules of the company require two guards with a train of more than 10 vehicles; but I had not a man at my disposal, and Clarke, who was to act as guard, stated that he could manage the train, as the rear brake van would be one of our most powerful vans".

The next witness was Samuel Clarke, a foreman porter at Cromer who had acted as a guard for four years; he agreed with station master Benns that he had felt confident enough to manage the train by himself with just one brake van, because "the van which would be in the rear was one of the large new heavy vans . . . with blocks on each wheel".

Walter Green, the driver of the train, was clearly an important witness. He had taken the excursion from Cromer to North Walsham, but was unsure if there were one or two guards aboard. However, he knew that there was "a good brake van" at the rear and had not been unduly perturbed at the thought of running with just one guard. Neither did he bother to fill the back sand boxes on his engine because he "did not expect to want it". The hand brake, he said, applied to the four coupled wheels of his 0–4–4 tank locomotive. Driver Green then described the events that had taken place after he had left North Walsham at 12.17 pm:

> We stopped at Gunton, without over-running, for collecting tickets. After leaving Gunton we ran at our usual speed, and I shut off steam about 300 yards on the Norwich side of the distant signal; this was about 300 yards sooner than usual, on account of the weight of the train and the state of the rails, which were greasy from drizzling rain, the speed being, I think, not more than 25 miles an hour. About 100 yards this side of the distant signal I told the fireman to apply the brake; this was also about 300 yards sooner than customary, for a similar reason to my shutting off steam earlier than usual. I thought I had the train fully in hand until I passed the signal cabin, when the engine wheels began to skid instead of revolving slowly, the speed being about 5 miles an hour. On seeing this I went to the brake myself, and just released it and applied it again, but the wheels again skidded, and I did not ease it again, but I jumped off on to the ballast in front of the driving wheels. It had little effect before the engine struck the empty carriages at a speed of about 3 miles an hour. I saw the dock signal off just on passing the distant signal; before seeing this I had not known whether I should run into the dock or on to the main line. I first saw the carriages in the dock when 50 or 60 yards from the cabin. I think if I had had sand in the back sand boxes I should have stopped without difficulty. It had not rained until after we had left North Walsham. I whistled for the station when shutting off steam, but I did not give the brake whistle, and have no reason to suppose the guard was not using his brake properly. I have only on two previous occasions run into the dock. I could have turned my engine at Cromer before starting, had I thought it would have rained. The engine was not damaged, and I took the 2 o'clock train to Norwich.

The final witness, fireman Daniel Todd, added that there was "no apprehension about stopping" until the train had passed Cromer signal box – at which point driver Green had eased the brake and put it on again before jumping down onto the ballast; he though that the train was travelling at "a speed of about 4 miles an hour" when it struck the stationary carriages.

Having considered the evidence, the BoT Inspector decided that the accident was "due primarily to want of judgment on the part of Walter Green, the driver of the train, in over-estimating his power of stopping a heavy train on a falling gradient with a comparatively small amount of brake power and the rails greasy from drizzling rain". The Major also criticised station master Benns for despatching the train with only one guard, while, on a more constructive note, he added that continuous brakes "would have been of the greatest service in enabling the driver to rectify his mistake" (Major General Hutchinson repeated this recommendation – with much greater force – after eighty travellers had lost their lives in the disastrous Armagh accident on 12th June, 1889; as a result of this accident, Paraliament at last acted to make continuous brakes compulsory on all British railways).

Sources for Chapter Two

16 *Kellys Directory of Norfolk.*
17 *Bradshaw's Shareholders' Manuals.*
18 *The Journal of the House of Commons; Bradhsaw's Shareholders' Manual.*
19 Dates taken from C.J. Allen, *The Great Eastern Railway* (1955).
20 V.L. Whitechurch, *The Railway Magazine*, June 1898 p.511
21 G.A. Sekon, Railways in Poppyland, *The Railway Magazine*, September 1904
22 *Ibid.* p.193
23 William Marriott, *Forty Years of a Norfolk Railway* (reprinted 1974).
24 *Ibid.*
25 E.L. Ahrons, Locomotive & Train Working in the Latter Part of the 19th Century, *The Railway Magazine*, 1918 *passim.*
26 E.L. Ahrons, *The Railway Magazine*, 1918, p.88
27 *Ibid.* p.89
28 *Ibid.* p.242
29 BoT Accident Report, 31st August, 1881.
30 *The Locomotive Magazine*, April 1907.

A Claud Hamilton 4–4–0 stands in the main platform at Cromer High (GER) station.
Lens of Sutton

EAST NORFOLK LINE.

NORWICH, WROXHAM, NORTH WALSHAM, MUNDESLEY-ON-SEA, OVERSTRAND, SHERINGHAM, AND CROMER.

DOWN TRAINS. — WEEK DAYS.

Reference to other Tables. Page.	DOWN TRAINS.	morn		morn		morn			morn		morn	
74-77 / 106 112	LONDON (Liverpool St. dep	...	...	5 5	...	5 33		...	10 0	...	10 0	...
	LONDON (St. Pancras "	—	—	—	—	—		—	9 15	—	9 15	—
74-77	Cambridge "	...	...	6 47	...	8 15		...	10 52	...	10 52	...
85	York "	—	—	—	—	—		—	...	—	...	—
	Doncaster "	...	...	...	...	...		...	8 0	...	8 0	...
	Lincoln "	—	—	—	—	—		—	9 5	—	9 5	—
94	Peterborough "	...	...	...	...	7 14		...	9 30	...	9 30	...
74-77	Ely "	—	—	7 8	—	8 47		—	11 18	—	11 18	—
95	Lynn "	...	...	...	...	8 51		...	10B20	...	10B20	...
99	Fakenham "	—	—	7Z35	—	9 38		—	10 21	—	10 21	—
	Dereham "	...	...	8Z4	...	10 8		...	10 50	...	10 50	...
106 112	Ipswich "	—	—	7 1	—	9 8		—	12 0	—	12 0	—
—	"	...	...	...	...	...		...	...	...	...	...
102	Yarmouth (Vaux.) dep.	6 40	—	7 35	—	10T5		—	12 0	—	12 57	—
	Lowestoft (Central) "	6N27	...	7 0	...	10 1		...	11E19	...	12 48	...
	NORWICH (Thorpe) dep.	7 15	—	9 5	—	11 18	11 30	—	1 25	—	1 44	—
	Whittlingham, *for Thorpe S. Andrew*	7 21	...	9 10	...	11 24	11 36	...	...	...	1 51	...
	Salhouse	7 30	—	9 19	—	11 33	11 45	—	—	—	1 59	—
	Wroxham	7 37	...	9 27	...	11 39	11 50	...	1 40	...	2 7	...
100	Wroxham dep.	7 42	—	—	—	—	11 51	—	—	—	2 11	—
	Coltishall arr.	7 48	...	...	...	...	11 57	...	...	...	2 17	...
	Buxton Lamas "	7 54	—	—	—	—	12 3	—	—	—	2 23	—
	Aylsham "	8 1	...	...	...	...	12 10	...	...	...	2 30	...
	Cawston "	8 11	—	—	—	—	12A20	—	—	—	2 40	—
	Reepham "	8 15	...	...	...	...	12A24	...	...	...	2 44	...
	Foulsham "	8 25	—	—	—	—	12A34	—	—	—	2 58	—
	County School "	8 33	...	...	...	...	12A42	...	...	...	3 7	...
	Worstead	7 46	—	9 34	—	11 48	—	—	—	—	2 16	—
	North Walsham (G.E.)	7 55	...	9 41	...	11 55	...	...	1 53	...	2 24	...
105	North Walsham (G.E.) dep.	8 18	—	10 32	—	S	—	—	2 45	—	2 45	—
	North Walsham (M.&G.N.) "	...	...	...	...	1 0	...	...	...	...	...	...
	N.S.C. Paston and Knapton arr.	8 27	—	10 41	—	1 8	—	—	2 53	—	2 53	—
	N.S.C. Mundesley-on-Sea "	8 32	...	10 46	...	1 12	...	...	2 57	...	2 57	...
	N.S.C. Trimingham "	8 57	—	11 7	—	1 19	—	—	3 5	—	3 5	—
	N.S.C. Overstrand "	9 3	...	11 12	...	1 26	...	...	3 10	...	3 10	...
106	Gunton	8 8	—	9 50	—	12 4	—	—	...	—	2 31	—
	West Runton arr.	8 30	...	10 11	...		...	...	2F28	...	...	...
	Sheringham "	8 33	—	10 14	—		—	—	2F31	—		—
	CROMER (G.E.) "	8 19	...	10 0	...	12 13	...	...	3 9	...	2 43	...

DOWN TRAINS.	noon (Not Saturdays. commences 2nd November.)	Not on Saturdays. Will commence running 2nd November.	even.	Not on Saturdays. Will run during October only.	even. (Saturdays only.)	During October Restaurant Cars will run on this Train from London to Cromer.	noon		even.	Will run daily during October afterwards on Saturdays only.
LONDON (Liverpool St. dep	12 0		1 30		1 30		12C0	...	1 30	
LONDON (St. Pancras "	12 20		12 25		12 20		12 20	—	12 20	
Cambridge "	1 37		1 37		1 37		1 37	...	1 37	
York "	10 25		10 25		10 25		10 25	—	10 25	
Doncaster "	11 16		11 16		11 16		11 16	...	11 16	
Lincoln "	12 9		12 9		12 9		12 9	—	12 9	
Peterborough "	12 52		12 52		12 52		12 52	...	12 52	
Ely "	2 6		2 6		2 6		2 6	—	2 6	
Lynn "	12 30		12 30		12 30		12 30	...	12 30	
Fakenham "	2 30		2 30		2 30		2 30	—	2 30	
Dereham "	2 57		2 57		2 57		2 57	...	2 57	
Ipswich "	—		3 4		3 4		3V4	—	3 4	
"	...		...		...		...	...	...	
Yarmouth (Vaux.) dep.	3 15		3 15		3 15		3 15	—	3 40	
Lowestoft (Central) "	2 53		2 53		2 53		2 53	...	3 30	
NORWICH (Thorpe) dep.	4 5		4 11		4 11		4 16	—	4 25	
Whittlingham, *for Thorpe S. Andrew*	...		...		H		...	...	4 31	
Salhouse	4 17		—				—	—	4 39	
Wroxham	4 23		4 26		4 26		4 31	...	4 45	
Wroxham dep.			—				4 32	—	—	
Coltishall arr.			...				4 38	...	...	
Buxton Lamas "			—				4 41	—	—	
Aylsham "			H				4 51	...	H	
Cawston "			—				5 1	—		
Reepham "			...				5 5	...	...	
Foulsham "			—				5 15	—	—	
County School "			...				5 23	...	...	
Worstead	4 32		—		—		—	—	4 54	
North Walsham (G.E.)	4 39		4 40		4 40		...	...	5 1	
North Walsham (G.E.) dep.	4 47		4 47		4 47		—	—	—	
North Walsham (M.&G.N.) "	...		...		...		...	...	...	
N.S.C. Paston and Knapton arr.	4 55		4 55		4 55		—	—	—	
N.S.C. Mundesley-on-Sea "	4 59		4 59		4 59		...	...	...	
N.S.C. Trimingham "	5 43		5 43		5 43		—	—	—	
N.S.C. Overstrand "	5 54		5 54		5 54		...	...	...	
Gunton	4 47		—		—		—	—	5 10	
West Runton arr.	...		...		5 12		...	...	...	
Sheringham "	—		—		5 15		—	—	—	
CROMER (G.E.) "	4 56		4 56		4 56		...	...	5 19	

DOWN TRAINS.	even.		even.		even.	Restaurant Cars—London to Cromer.	even.		
LONDON (Liverpool St. dep	3 20	...	3 20	...	4 55		5 12	...	...
LONDON (St. Pancras "	—	—	2 40	—	—		5 5	—	—
Cambridge "	...	...	4 6	...	...		6 36	...	...
York "	—	—	12 50	—	—		—	—	—
Doncaster "	...	...	1 42	...	H		...	...	...
Lincoln "	—	—	2 37	—			—	—	—
Peterborough "	...	...	3 30	...	...		4 58	...	...
Ely "	—	—	4 37	—	—		7 9	—	—
Lynn "	3 11	...	4 53	...	5 43		...	...	...
Fakenham "	3 46	—	3D46	—	6 18		—	—	—
Dereham "	4 17	...	5 51	...	6 51		...	...	...
Ipswich "	4 55	—	5 5	—	6 28		—	—	—
"	...	...	...	...	...		...	...	...
Yarmouth (Vaux.) dep.	5 8	—	6 5	—	—		7 22	—	—
Lowestoft (Central) "	...	...	5 48	...	...		...	...	...
NORWICH (Thorpe) dep.	6 5	—	6 45	—	8 2		9 10	—	—
Whittlingham, *for Thorpe S. Andrew*	6 11	...	6 52	...	...		9 16	...	...
Salhouse	6 20	—	7 1	—	—		9 25	—	—
Wroxham	6 29	...	7 8	...	8 18		9 32	...	...
Wroxham dep.	—	—	7 12	—	—		9 35	—	—
Coltishall arr.	...	...	7 18	...	...		9 41	...	...
Buxton Lamas "	—	—	7 24	—	—		9 47	—	—
Aylsham "	...	...	7 31	...	...		9 54	...	...
Cawston "	—	—	7 41	—	—		10 4	—	—
Reepham "	...	...	7 45	...	...		10 8	...	...
Foulsham "	—	—	—	—	—		10 17	—	—
County School "	...	...	...	...	...		...	...	...
Worstead	—	—	7 17	—	—		9 41	—	—
North Walsham (G.E.)	6 42	...	7 24	...	8 34		9 48	...	...
North Walsham (G.E.) dep.	6 45	—	S	—	—		—	—	—
North Walsham (M.&G.N.) "	...	...	7 55	...	...		...	...	...
N.S.C. Paston and Knapton arr.	6 52	—	8 3	—	—		—	—	—
N.S.C. Mundesley-on-Sea "	6 55	...	8 7	...	...		...	...	...
N.S.C. Trimingham "	7 7	—	...	—	—		—	—	—
N.S.C. Overstrand "	7 12	...	—	...	...		...	...	...
Gunton	...	—	7 32	—	—		9 56	—	—
West Runton arr.	7 14	...	...	...	9L1		...	...	...
Sheringham "	7 17	—	—	—	9L4		—	—	—
CROMER (G.E.) "	6 58	...	7 42	...	8 48		10 5	...	...

SUNDAYS.

DOWN TRAINS.	morn (Will run during October only. / Runs during October only.)	morn	even.	even.			
LONDON (Liverpool St. dep	...	9 50	...	3 30	...	...	...
LONDON (St. Pancras "	—	—	—	—	—	—	—
Cambridge "	...	11 18	...	5 0	...	...	...
York "		—	—	—	—	—	—
Doncaster "		...	...	2 35	...	...	...
Lincoln "		—	—	3 33	—	—	—
Peterborough "		...	...	4 40	...	...	...
Ely "		11 42	—	5 33	—	—	—
Lynn "		...	...	3G25	...	...	...
Fakenham "		—	5 22	—	—	—	—
Dereham "		...	5 53	...	...	...	...
Ipswich "	—	—	—	—	—	—	—
"	...	...	...	...	...	...	...
Yarmouth (Vaux.) dep.	9 5	1 20	6 0	—		—	—
Lowestoft (Central) "	8 58	1 12	5 47	...		...	...
NORWICH (Thorpe) dep.	10 10	2 10	6 52	9 10	—	—	—
Whittlingham, *for Thorpe S. Andrew*	10 16	2 16	6 58	9 16	...	...	...
Salhouse	10 25	2 25	7 6	9 25	—	—	—
Wroxham	10 32	2 32	7 12	9 32	...	...	...
Wroxham dep.		—	—	—	—	—	—
Coltishall arr.		...	...	...	...	...	...
Buxton Lamas "		—	—	—	—	—	—
Aylsham "		...	...	...	...	...	...
Cawston "		—	—	—	—	—	—
Reepham "		...	...	...	...	...	...
Foulsham "		—	—	—	—	—	—
County School "		...	...	...	...	...	...
Worstead	10 41	2 41	7 21	9 41	—	—	—
North Walsham (G.E.)	10 48	2 48	7 28	9 48	...	...	...
North Walsham (G.E.) dep.	—	—	—	—	—	—	—
North Walsham (M.&G.N.) "	...	...	...	...	...	...	...
N.S.C. Paston and Knapton arr.	—	—	—	—	—	—	—
N.S.C. Mundesley-on-Sea "	...	...	...	...	...	...	...
N.S.C. Trimingham "	—	—	—	—	—	—	—
N.S.C. Overstrand "	...	...	...	...	...	...	...
Gunton	10 56	2 56	7 36	9 56	—	—	—
West Runton arr.	...	...	...	...	...	...	...
Sheringham "	—	—	—	—	—	—	—
CROMER (G.E.) "	11 5	3 5	7 45	10 5	...	...	...

A On Thursdays and Fridays due at Cawston 12.54 p.m., Reepham 12.58, Foulsham 1.9, and County School at 1 17 p.m.
B From Lynn on Saturdays only.
C On Saturdays leaves Liverpool Street 1.30 p.m., during October will leave at 1.30 p.m. every Week-day.
D From Fakenham at 5.10 p.m. on Thursdays.
E Saturdays only.
F On Mondays arrives at West Runton 2.20 and Sheringham 2.23 p.m. During October these times will apply each Week-day.
G Via Ely.
H Horses and Private Carriages not conveyed by these Trains.

L Runs to West Runton and Sheringham on Fridays only.
N Mondays only, and will run during October only.
S Passengers for Paston and Knapton, Mundesley-on-Sea, Trimingham, and Overstrand by these Trains require to cross from the Great Eastern to the Mid. & G.N. Joint Company's Station at North Walsham.
T Commencing 2nd November will leave Yarmouth at 10.10 a.m.
V From Ipswich on Saturdays only, during October will run every Week-day
Z On Mondays leaves Fakenham 6.35 a.m. and Dereham 7.4 a.m.

For particulars of Through Carriages see pages 204 and 205.

The Passenger Timetable of the East Norfolk Line for 1908.

EAST NORFOLK LINE.

CROMER, SHERINGHAM, OVERSTRAND, MUNDESLEY-ON-SEA, NORTH WALSHAM, WROXHAM, AND NORWICH.

UP TRAINS. — WEEK DAYS.

Reference to other Tables. Page.	UP TRAINS.	morn			W morn (Restaurant Cars—Cromer to London.)	morn		morn	Z morn		even.		ZZ even. (Will run daily during October afterwards on Mondays only.)
105	CROMER (G.E.) dep.	6 23		...	8 0	8A45	...	...	10 0	...	12 35	...	1 13
	Sheringham "	—		—	7 34	—	—	—	9 42	—	—	—	1 0
	West Runton "	...		...	7 38	...	...	...	9 46	...	...	...	1 4
	Gunton "	6 32		—	—	8A54	—	—	10 13	—	12 44	—	—
105	M. & G. J. Overstrand dep.	...		...	7 22	...	...	...	9 42	...	12 6	...	...
	Trimingham "	—		—	7 28	—	—	—	9 48	—	12 14	—	—
	Mundesley-on-Sea "	...		...	7 35	...	...	...	9 55	...	12 22	...	...
	Paston and Knapton "	—		—	7 39	—	—	—	9 59	—	12 26	—	—
	North Walsham (M. & G.N.) arr.	...		...	...	...	...	...	...	...	12 31	...	...
	North Walsham (G.E.) "	—		—	7 47	—	—	—	10 7	—	S	—	—
	North Walsham (G.E.)	6 40		...	8 13	9A2	...	...	10 21	...	12 52	...	1 30
	Worstead	6 46		—	—	9A8	—	—	10 27	—	12 58	—	—
100	County School dep.	...		...	...	...	...	9 25	...	...	12 5	...	...
	Foulsham	—		—	7 20	—	—	9 33	—	—	12 13	—	—
	Reepham	...		...	7 29	...	...	9 42	...	...	12 25	...	...
	Cawston	—		—	7 34	—	—	9 47	—	—	12 30	—	ZZ
	Aylsham	...		...	7 44	...	...	9 56	Z	...	12 39	...	...
	Buxton Lamas	—		—	8 2	—	—	10 3	—	—	12 46	—	—
	Coltishall	...		...	8 8	...	...	10 9	...	...	12 52	...	...
	Wroxham arr.	—		—	8 13	—	—	10 15	—	—	12 58	—	—
	Wroxham dep.	6 55		...	8 26	9A19	...	10 17	10 36	...	1 9	...	1 42
	Salhouse	7 2		—	—	9A26	—	10 24	—	—	1 16	—	—
	Whitlingham for Thorpe S. Andrew	7 11		...	W	9A35	...	10 33	...	...	1 25	...	...
	NORWICH (Thorpe) arr.	7 16		—	8 41	9A40	—	10 40	10 50	—	1 30	—	1 57
101	Lowestoft (Central) arr.	8 8		...	10L2	11C14	...	12 13		...	2 31	...	...
	Yarmouth (Vaux.) "	8 3		—	9 57	10 39	—	12 8		—	2 26	—	3B30
113 119	Ipswich arr.	—	9 4	—	9 41	11 54	—	1 16		—	4X47	—	2 59
99	Dereham "	8 59	H	...	...	11 28	...	1 47		...	4 17	...	4 17
	Fakenham "	9 34		—	—	11 57	—	2 19		—	4 49	—	4 49
96	Lynn "	9 52		...	...	12H21	...	2 50		...	5 18	...	5 18
78-82	Ely "	9 6		—	—	—	—	12 48		—	4 2	—	4 2
93	Peterborough "	10 5		...	...	...	...	1 45		...	5 52	...	5 52
83	Lincoln "	10 57	Mondays only.	—	—	—	—	2 32		—	—	—	—
	Doncaster "	11 48		...	...	...	...	3 26		...	...	...	...
	York "	12 35		—	—	—	—	4 25		—	—	—	—
78, 82	Cambridge "	9 40		...	...	...	...	1 16		...	4 31	...	4 34
78 82	LONDON St. Pancras "	11 15		—	--	—	—	2 43		—	6 10	—	6 10
113 119	LONDON Liverpool St. "	11 10	10 45	...	11 25	2 25	...	2 49		...	6X6	...	4 50

UP TRAINS. — WEEK DAYS (continued).

UP TRAINS.	ZZ even.		even.		FT even.		U even.		FV even.		P even.					
CROMER (G.E.) dep.	2 35	...	...	...	2T58	...	5U20	...	5V55	...	8 15	...	...	...	...	...
Sheringham "	2D0	—	—	—	2F36	—	5R9	—	5F5	—	8P0	—	—	—	—	—
West Runton "	2D4	...	...	...	2F40	...	5R13	...	5F39	...	8P4	...	...	...	...	...
Gunton "	2 34	—	—	—	3 7	—	5 35	—	6 4	—	8 24	—	—	—	—	—
Overstrand dep.	2 2	...	...	...	...	...	4 56	...	...	...	7 1	...	...	...	...	...
Trimingham "	2 8	—	—	—	—	—	5 2	—	—	—	7 8	—	—	—	—	—
Mundesley-on-Sea "	2 15	...	...	...	...	...	5 20	...	...	...	7 15	...	...	...	...	...
Paston and Knapton "	2 19	—	—	—	—	—	5 24	—	—	—	7 19	—	—	—	—	—
North Walsham (M. & G.N.) arr.	—	...	...	...	...	...	...	...	...	...	7 27	...	...	...	...	...
North Walsham (G.E.) "	2 27	—	—	—	—	—	5 32	—	—	—	S	—	—	—	—	—
North Walsham (G.E.)	2 42	...	...	...	3 15	...	5 42	...	6 12	...	8 32	...	...	...	...	...
Worstead	—	—	—	—	3 21	—	5 48	—	6 18	—	8 38	—	—	—	—	—
County School dep.	...	...	2 30	...	...	...	...	...	5 30	...	...	...	...	...	...	...
Foulsham	—	—	2 38	—	—	—	—	—	5 38	—	—	—	—	—	—	—
Reepham	...	...	2 49	...	...	...	...	...	5 48	...	8 5	...	...	...	...	...
Cawston	ZZ	—	2 54	—	—	—	H	—	5 53	—	8 10	—	—	—	—	—
Aylsham	...	...	3 3	...	...	...		...	6 2	...	8 19	...	...	...	...	...
Buxton Lamas	—	—	3 10	—	—	—	—	—	6 9	—	8 26	—	—	—	—	—
Coltishall	...	...	3 16	...	...	...	...	...	6 15	...	8 32	...	...	...	...	...
Wroxham arr.	—	—	3 22	—	—	—	—	—	6 21	—	8 38	—	—	—	—	—
Wroxham dep.	2 56	...	3 23	...	3 32	...	5 57	...	6 30	...	8 49	...	...	...	...	...
Salhouse	—	—	3 30	—	3 39	—	6 4	—	6 37	—	8 56	—	—	—	—	—
Whitlingham for Thorpe S. Andrew	...	...	3 39	...	3 48	...	...	...	6 45	...	9 5	...	...	...	...	...
NORWICH (Thorpe) arr.	3 12	—	3 44	—	3 53	—	6 14	—	6 50	—	9 10	—	—	—	—	—
Lowestoft (Central) arr.	4E32	...	5 19	...	5 19	...	7 54	...	7 54	...	10 17	...	...	...	...	...
Yarmouth (Vaux.) "	---	—	4 50	—	4 50	—	7 18	—	7 48	—	10 11	—	—	—	—	—
Ipswich arr.	4 47	—	—	—	—	—	7 32	—	—	—	—	—	—	—	—	—
Dereham "	4 17	...	4 38	...	4 38	...	7 12	...	7 42	...	...	...	...	...	...	...
Fakenham "	4 49	—	7K12	—	7K12	—	7 42	—	8 35	—	—	—	—	—	—	—
Lynn "	5 18	...	5 30	...	5 30	...	8 45	...	8 45	...	...	...	...	...	...	...
Ely "	—	—	6 28	—	6 26	—	8 55	—	8 55	—	12 13	—	—	—	—	—
Peterborough "	...	...	6 41	...	6 41	...	...	...	...	...	1 43	...	...	...	...	...
Lincoln "	—	—	8 7	—	8 7	—	—	—	—	—	—	—	—	—	—	—
Doncaster "	...	...	9 2	...	9 2	...	...	...	...	...	...	...	...	...	...	...
York "	—	—	9 54	—	9 54	—	—	—	—	—	morn	—	—	—	—	—
Cambridge "	...	...	6 55	...	6 55	...	9 27	...	9 27	...	12 45	...	...	...	...	...
LONDON St. Pancras "	—	—	8 35	—	8 35	—	—	—	—	—	—	—	—	—	—	—
LONDON Liverpool St. "	6 40	...	8 26	...	8 26	...	9 25	...	...	...	3 0	...	...	...	...	...

UP TRAINS. — SUNDAYS.

UP TRAINS.	morn	even.	even.		even.	even. (Will run during October only. Restaurant Cars - Cromer to London.)
CROMER (G.E.) dep.	8 55	1 0	5 10	...	5 45	8 0
Sheringham "	—	—	—	—	—	—
West Runton "	...	...	...	...	...	...
Gunton "	9 4	1 9	5 19	—	—	8 9
Overstrand dep.	...	...	...	...	...	...
Trimingham "	—	—	—	—	—	—
Mundesley-on-Sea "	...	...	...	...	...	...
Paston and Knapton "	—	—	—	—	—	—
North Walsham (M. & G.N.) arr.	...	...	...	...	...	...
North Walsham (G.E.) "	—	—	—	—	—	—
North Walsham (G.E.)	9 12	1 17	5 27	...	5 59	8 17
Worstead	9 18	1 23	5 33	—	—	8 23
County School dep.	Runs during October only.	...	...	...	Runs during October only.	...
Foulsham		—	—	—		—
Reepham		...	...	...		...
Cawston		—	—	—		—
Aylsham		...	...	...		...
Buxton Lamas		—	—	—		—
Coltishall		...	...	...		...
Wroxham arr.		—	—	—		—
Wroxham dep.	9 27	1 32	5 42	...	6 11	8 32
Salhouse	9 34	1 39	5 49	—	H	8 39
Whitlingham for Thorpe S. Andrew	9 43	1 45	5 58	...		8 48
NORWICH (Thorpe) arr.	9 48	1 53	6 3	—	6 25	8 53
Lowestoft (Central) arr.	10 47	3 0	8 30	...	8 30	10 17
Yarmouth (Vaux.) "	10 43	2 55	8 24	...	8 24	10 11
Ipswich arr.	Runs during October only.	—	7J28	—	7 28	—
Dereham "		...	7 57	...	7 57	...
Fakenham "		—	8 27	—	8 27	—
Lynn "		G20	...	...	...	...
Ely "		4 2	7 41	—	—	12 13
Peterborough "		6 52	...	...	...	1 43
Lincoln "		—	—	—	—	—
Doncaster "		...	...	...	...	...
York "		—	—	—	—	morn
Cambridge "		5 0	8 11	...	...	12 45
LONDON St. Pancras "	—	...	9 41	—	—	—
LONDON Liverpool St. "	...	6 26	9Y37	...	9 15	3 0

A During October will run 5 minutes later.
B To Yarmouth on Mondays, Thursdays, and Saturdays only, and will run during October only.
C Mondays only, and will run during October only.
D Will commence running 3rd November, and will not run from Sheringham and West Runton on Mondays.
E Saturdays only.
F Runs from Sheringham and West Runton on Saturdays only.
G Via Ely.
H Horses and Private Carriages not conveyed by these Trains.
J Will run during October only.
K Due at Fakenham at 6.16 p.m. on Tuesdays and at 6.10 p.m. on Saturdays.
L During October will arrive at Lowestoft 9.55 a.m.
N To Lynn on Tuesdays only. **P** Runs from Sheringham and West Runton on Fridays only.
R Does not run from Sheringham and West Runton on Saturdays.
S Passengers from Overstrand, Trimingham, Mundesley-on-Sea, and Paston and Knapton require to cross from the Mid. & G.N. Joint to the Great Eastern Company's Station at North Walsham.
T On Saturdays leaves Cromer at 2.54 p.m. **U** On Saturdays leaves Cromer at 5.24 p.m.
V On Saturdays leaves Cromer at 5.52 p.m.
W Does not convey Horses and Private Carriages except from Cromer to Liverpool Street.
X On Mondays arrives at Ipswich 2.59 and Liverpool Street 4.50 p.m., during October will arrive at these times daily.
Y During October will arrive at Liverpool Street 9.15 p.m.
Z Does not convey Horses and Private Carriages except from Cromer and Sheringham for St. Pancras and from Sheringham for Liverpool Street.
ZZ Does not convey Horses and Private Carriages except from Cromer and Sheringham for Liverpool Street.

For particulars of Through Carriages see pages 204 and 205.

Chapter Three

The "Poppyland" Era (1906–1923)

The Edwardian era was the golden age of Cromer and its railways, and with more and more people visiting the area each year the town seemed to have an assured future as a rather select middle class resort; in fact, of all Norfolk resorts, only the more egalitarian watering place of Great Yarmouth exceeded Cromer in popularity.

The resort's undoubted success inevitably resulted in many changes and improvements to the local railway system, and in addition to the new loops and junctions provided at Cromer in connection with the Norfolk & Suffolk Joint line, the branch benefited from the installation of double track between Whitlingham Junction and Wroxham in 1896, followed by a further doubling between Worstead and North Walsham in 1901. From North Walsham to Cromer Junction the line remained single, but in 1906 a further section of double track was installed between Cromer Junction and Cromer GER station, thereby increasing line capacity at this northernmost extremity of the route.

The doubling of the line between Whitlingham and North Walsham led, in turn, to improvements at the intermediate stations of Salhouse, North Walsham and Worstead – all of which gained extra facilities in the form of new waiting rooms and other accommodation. Elsewhere, there was much investment in signalling equipment, signal boxes, and other new facilities, and by the end of the 19th century the branch had been fully equipped with standard Great Eastern signals.

The single line section between North Walsham and Cromer Junction was controlled by electric train tablet, with Gunton as a crossing and tablet station, while the single track Norfolk & Suffolk Joint line from North Walsham to Roughton Road Junction was similarly equipped. All but one of its stations were passing places, and in the Edwardian period the line was divided into the following block sections: Roughton Road Junction–Overstrand, Overstrand–Trimingham, Trimingham–Mundesley, and Mundesley–Antingham Road Junction.

At the turn-of-the-century the Cromer branch was still worked by trains composed mainly of short wheelbase stock, but in the years before World War I there was a gradual increase in the proportion of bogie stock relative to six-wheelers.

Until 1904 the Great Eastern Railway had no complete trains of corridor stock, but the company had initiated a policy of adding bogie restaurant cars to its most prestigious trains. These vehicles were coupled together in three-coach sets, and it was usual for each self-contained restaurant car set to be marshalled with non-vestibuled six-wheelers so that, in the early years of the century, Great Eastern expresses were typically composed of both short wheelbase *and* bogie stock. Restaurant cars were at first included only in the prestigious Hook of Holland boat train, but in 1899 the GER constructed four new restaurant car sets for use on Cromer and Yarmouth services, and by the turn-of-the-century Cromer residents were enjoying the advantages of an all-year-round restaurant car service to London.

Residential Traffic

It should be stressed that until the widespread introduction of holidays with pay, resorts such as Cromer were *residential towns* rather than holiday centres, and although cheap tickets encouraged ordinary folk to spend odd days by the seaside, the patrons of Edwardian Cromer were predominantly middle class businessmen who actually lived in the town for all or part of the year.

To explain why these individuals chose to reside in places such as Cromer it is worth remembering that rail travel enabled people to commute to and from London or other places of business. Although the thought of spending up to six hours a day travelling to work may now seem rather harrowing, one might add that many businessmen and industrialists were happy to travel such long distances – not only to Cromer but to scores of similar resorts around the British coastline. It became, in many ways, a mark of status to live away from the smoke-laden cities in which wealth was created – and the further away that one lived the greater was the aura of wealth and success. Ultra-successful businessmen might even purchase a country estate and "retreat" from industrial society altogether, but few could ever hope for this final accolade, and under the circumstances large numbers of comparatively wealthy travellers were content to live in seaside towns such as Cromer, Hunstanton or Frinton-on-Sea.

One might also remember that many of the people who lived in Cromer while travelling to work in the City would probably not have to travel every day, while at the same time others would no doubt have lived in clubs, apartments or other accommodation in London during the week, and travelled to Cromer only at weekends. Alternatively, a wealthy Edwardian could have hired rooms in Cromer for the summer so that his wife and children were able to live by the sea while he remained in the City; the permutations were endless, but suffice to say there was considerable "commuter" traffic to and from Cromer throughout the year, and for this reason the Great Eastern was keen to provide the best possible express train services between Cromer and London.

The "Cromer Express"

When the railway was first opened, journeys from Cromer to London had taken about four and a half hours, but these leisurely timings were progressively improved as Cromer gained in popularity as a long distance commuter resort. On 3rd November, 1895 the Great Eastern operating authorities carried out an interesting experiment in which Holden oil-fired 2–2–2 No. 1006 successfully ran non-stop between London and Cromer, with an eight-coach train consisting of 6 short-wheelbase coaches and two new bogie vehicles. The 138 mile journey was accomplished on just one 3,100 gallon tender full of water, but the experiment had shown that such runs were impracticable unless locomotives could replenish their stock of water *en route*, and in 1896 the Great Eastern provided a set of water troughs at Tivetshall for that purpose.

GO TO THE

BRACING EAST COAST

BY THE

G.E.R.

FOR YOUR

SUMMER HOLIDAYS.

CROMER
OVERSTRAND
TRIMINGHAM
MUNDESLEY
SHERINGHAM
WEST RUNTON
YARMOUTH
LOWESTOFT
GORLESTON
HUNSTANTON
ALDEBURGH
SOUTHWOLD
FELIXSTOWE
CLACTON
WALTON
FRINTON
HARWICH
DOVERCOURT
SOUTHEND
and the
NORFOLK BROADS

ABUNDANT AMUSEMENTS.	BRACING BREEZES.	CHARMING COUNTRY.

FAST TRAINS.
CHEAP TICKETS.

CORRIDOR CARRIAGES.
RESTAURANT CARS.

YACHTING. FISHING. MAGNIFICENT GOLF LINKS.

RAIL and BOAT EXCURSIONS.

Descriptive Pamphlets and full particulars sent gratis on application to the Superintendent of the Line, Liverpool Street Station, E.C.

A CALL
TO THE
EAST
COAST
GREAT EASTERN RLY.

G.E.R.

CHEAP FARES and - -
COMFORTABLE TRAVEL

TO THE

SUNNY EAST COAST

FOR THE

HOLIDAYS.

ABUNDANT AMUSEMENT

BRACING BREEZES

CHARMING COUNTRY

A SELECTION OF **19** BRACING COAST RESORTS.

Frequent and Convenient Service of Fast Trains.

Non-Stop Trains.

Restaurant Car Expresses.

CHEAP TICKETS for Varying Periods.

LUGGAGE IN ADVANCE.

HUNSTANTON.
SHERINGHAM.
WEST RUNTON.
CROMER.
OVERSTRAND.
TRIMINGHAM.
MUNDESLEY-ON-SEA.
YARMOUTH.
GORLESTON-ON-SEA.
LOWESTOFT.
SOUTHWOLD.
ALDEBURGH.
FELIXSTOWE.
HARWICH.
DOVERCOURT.
WALTON-ON-NAZE
FRINTON-ON-SEA.
CLACTON-ON-SEA.
SOUTHEND-ON-SEA.

Magnificent Golf Links.

Extensive Sands & Promenades.

Charming Country for CYCLING, DRIVING and WALKING.

Angling & Yachting on the Norfolk Broads.

Etc., Etc.

Descriptive and Illustrated Guides, Programmes, and full information will be sent gratis upon application to the Superintendent of the Line, Liverpool Street Station, London, E.C.

Having demonstrated that non-stop running was a viable proposition, the GER next provided a fast Sunday express service from Cromer to Liverpool Street. This new train left the resort at 7.05 pm and reached London in the record time of 3 hours 25 minutes, enabling weekenders to be back in the capital in time for a full day's work on the following Monday.

A further development came in the summer of 1897 when a new, prestige train – known, appropriately enough, as "The Cromer Express" – was introduced between Liverpool Street and Cromer. Headed by a Holden 7 ft single, the "Cromer Express" covered the 130 miles between North Walsham and London in only 159 minutes, putting Cromer within 2 hours 55 minutes travelling time of the metropolis. The train ran non-stop from North Walsham to London, making use of the Wensum Curve which obviated the need to stop for reversal at Norwich Thorpe; there was also a new set of water troughs at Ipswich, and these were of greater use than the earlier Tivetshall troughs in that Ipswich was conveniently-placed at a midway position between Cromer and London.

When first introduced, on 1st July, 1897, the non-stop "Cromer Express" was headed by a 2–4–0, but Holden 2–2–2s had been used on London to Cromer workings in the previous year, and these locomotives – which were thought to be more "free running" than their coupled counterparts – were the type normally used on the best trains prior to 1900. Interestingly, both 2–4–0s and 2–2–2s were oil-fired, using Holden's patent system whereby waste products from the Great Eastern's gas works were burned on a "bed" of coal. V.L. Whitechurch recalled that, in 1897, the "Cromer Express" was:

> Regularly worked by the "single" express engines of Mr Holden's standard design, fired on his patent liquid fuel system. The chief dimensions of the engines used . . . were as follows: cylinders, 18 in. diameter by 24 in. stroke, and drivers 7 ft. diameter, with a boiler having 1,217 square feet of heating surface, and a working pressure of 160 lb. per square inch.[31]

The usual engines were Nos. 1004–1009, all of which had been equipped with water-scoop tenders and converted to oil-firing for service on the "Cromer Express". Locomotives used on this prestige service were based at Ipswich or Norwich sheds – the normal practice being for Ipswich or Norwich men to work "circular" diagrams between London, Ipswich, Norwich and Cromer. In theory, these relatively small locomotives hauled a ten-coach train, comprising one 6-wheeled brake, one 6-wheeled third, one 6-wheeled first, three bogie composites, two 6-wheeled thirds, one 6-wheeled brake and a 4-wheeled luggage van. When fully loaded, such a train would have weighed about 180 tons, but at the height of the season five (or even more) extra vehicles were regularly added, and V.L. Whitechurch claimed that the train sometimes consisted of "no less than seventeen vehicles".

Officially quoted figures suggest that the total *empty* weight of the "Cromer Express" could reach 270 tons 17 cwt, and these figures provide a useful supplement to V.L. Whitechurch's eye-witness account. Seventeen vehicles was the summer maximum, the usual formation being as follows:

		tons	cwt	qtr
1	6-wheeled brake van	12	11	00
2	6-wheeled third class coaches	26	18	00
2	6-wheeled third class coaches	26	12	00
1	6-wheeled first class coach	13	15	2¼
1	bogie first class corridor coach	23	05	02
1	bogie dining car	29	08	02
1	bogie third class corridor coach	27	10	01
1	bogie composite coach	21	04	00
1	6-wheeled first class coach	13	15	2¼
1	6-wheeled third class coach	13	09	00
1	6-wheeled brake van	12	11	00
1	6-wheeled composite coach	13	19	2½
1	6-wheeled third class coach	13	09	00
1	6-wheeled composite brake van	14	03	00
1	4-wheeled fruit van	08	05	00
TOTAL WEIGHT EMPTY		270	17	00

The Norfolk Coast Express

Holden's 2–2–2s were soon replaced by enlarged singles of the 'P43' class, and these 4–2–2s regularly handled mixed short-wheelbase and bogie formations weighing up to 300 tons. Meanwhile, the opening of the Norfolk & Suffolk Joint line with its connecting loops at Cromer enabled the Great Eastern to serve a wider range of destinations than had hitherto been possible, and in a desire to open-up the Mundesley area to holidaymakers (and potential residents) the GER added a Mundesley portion to the "Cromer Express". The train henceforth divided at North Walsham, from where eight coaches ran to Cromer High while two vehicles were worked over the Mundesley to Overstrand line, and two more continued over the M&GN to Sheringham. Total tare weight of the complete twelve-coach formation was about 317 tons, and as a result of the diverse destinations now provided for the train was, from 1907, re-christened the "Norfolk Coast Express".[32]

In 1908, the "Norfolk Coast Express" left London at 1 pm (in some years brought forward to 1.30 pm) and, running non-stop to North Walsham, it arrived in Cromer by 3.55 pm. In the opposite direction, the corresponding up train also departed from Cromer at 1 pm and drew to a stand at Liverpool Street just as its northbound counterpart was arriving in Cromer. The train was one of the most glamorous on the GER (indeed, to many travellers it was *the* most prestigious service) and every effort was made to keep good time on the 2 hour 55 minute journey; specially selected locomotives were maintained in excellent mechanical condition – and it is said that even the coal was carefully chosen to ensure an optimum performance![33] The crews, too, were probably among the best on the GER, and the exploits of drivers such as Harry Nudd of Norwich and Arthur Cage of Ipswich became legendary (there was, inevitably, a degree of healthy rivalry between men from Ipswich and Norwich sheds, and this factor possibly contributed to the sparkling performance that came to be expected on the "Norfolk Coast Express").

THE NORFOLK COAST EXPRESS

Schedule Times

MILES.	DOWN.				
—	Liverpool Street	dep.	1 30		
4	Stratford	pass.	1 39		
10	Chadwell Heath..	,,	1 46		
20¼	Shenfield	,,	1 59		
29¾	Ch lmsford	,,	2 9		
38¾	Witham	,,	2 19		
51¾	Colchester	,,	2 34		
59½	Manningtree	,,	2 43		
68¾	Ipswich	,,	2 53		
80¾	Stowmarket	,,	3 7		
83	Haughley	,,	3 10		
100½	Tivetshall	,,	3 30		
114	Trowse	,,	3 44		
114¾	Wensum Junction	,,	3 47		
130	North Walsham.. ..	arr.	4 8		
		dep.	4 12	4 17	4 22
130¼	North Walsham Junction	pass.	4 13	4 18	—
134	Gunton	,,	4 17	4 24	—
137½	Cromer Junction	,,	4 23	4 30	—
138¼	Cromer	arr.	4 25	—	—
141	West Runton	,,	—	4 38	—
142¾	Sheringham	,,	—	4 43	—
133½	Paston	,,	—	—	4 30
135¼	Mundesley	,,	—	—	4 34
137¾	Trimingham	,,	—	—	4 42
140¼	Overstrand	,,	—	—	4 48

UP.		p.m.	p.m.	p.m.
Overstrand	dep	12 32	—	—
Trimingham	,,	12 38	—	—
Mundesley	,,	12 47	—	—
Paston..	,,	12 51	—	—
Sheringham	,,	—	12 36	—
West Runton	,,	—	12 41	—
Cromer	,,	—	—	1 0
Cromer Junction	pass.	—	12 52	1 2
Gunton	,,	—	12 59	1 7
North Walsham Junction	,,	—	1 5	1 11
North Walsham.. ..	arr.	12 59	1 6	1 12
	dep.		1 16	
Wensum Junction	pass.		1 37	
Trowse	,,		1 40	
Tivetshall	,,		1 59	
Haughley	,,		2 18	
Stowmarket	,,		2 20	
Ipswich	,,		2 32	
Manningtree	,,		2 44	
Colchester	,,		2 54	
Witham	,,		3 9	
Chelmsford	,,		3 19	
Shenfield	,,		3 30	
Chadwell Heath..	,,		3 40	
Stratford	,,		3 47	
Liverpool Street	arr.		3 55	

The Norfolk Coast Express schedule times for 1908.

1.30 P.M. LIVERPOOL STREET TO CROMER.

Log of Journey, July 27th, 1908.
Engine 1871, 4–4–0 Type. Driver Cage.
Load—13 bogies =350 tons.

M.	C.			H.	M.	S.	Service Speed Reductions.
—		Liverpool Street.. ..	dep.	1	30	0	
	31	Bishopsgate	pass.	1	31	46	
1	18	Bethnal Green	,,	1	33	35	
1	60	Globe Road	,,	1	34	28	
2	27	Coborn Road	,,	1	35	28	
3	71	Stratford	,,	1	37	55	20m.p.h.
4	30	Maryland Point	,,	1	38	45	
5	12	Forest Gate	,,	1	39	57	
6	21	Manor Park	,,	1	41	34	
7	31	Ilford	,,	1	43	5	
8	55	Seven Kings	,,	1	44	45	
9	41	Goodmayes..	,,	1	45	47	
10	21	Chadwell Heath ..	,,	1	46	46	
12	25	Romford	,,	1	49	15	
15	1	Harold Wood	,,	1	52	30	
18	12	Brentwood	,,	1	57	43	
20	17	Shenfield	,,	2	1	27	
23	42	Ingatestone	,,	2	4	54	
29	64	Chelmsford	,,	2	10	40	30 m.p.h.
35	71	Hatfield Peveril ..	,,	2	17	50	
38	44	Witham	,,	2	20	40	
42	16	Kelvedon	,,	2	24	19	
46	54	Marks Tey	,,	2	29	31	
51	47	Colchester	,,	2	34	35	40 m.p.h.
56	6	Ardleigh	,,	2	39	47	
59	24	Manningtree	,,	2	43	15	
63	20	Bentley	,,	2	47	15	
68	57	Ipswich	,,	2	53	19	25 m.p.h.
71	20	Bramford	,,	2	56	50	
73	46	Claydon	,,	2	59	33	
76	11	Needham	,,	3	3	41	
80	51	Stowmarket	,,	3	7	46	
82	73	Haughley	,,	3	10	26	
86	45	Finningham	,,	3	16	6	
90	33	Mellis	,,	3	21	30	
95	1	Diss	,,	3	24	55	
97	42	Burston	,,	3	27	19	
100	43	Tivetshall	,,	3	30	55	
104	6	Forncett	,,	3	34	48	
106	56	Flordon	,,	3	37	7	
108	54	Swainsthorpe	,,	3	39	50	
112	67	Trowse Upper Junction	,,	3	42	42	15 m.p.h.
114	13	Trowse Station	,,	3	44	39	
114	35	Swing Bridge Junction	,,	3	45	15	15 m.p.h.
114	63	Wensum Junction ..	,,	3	46	39	
115	76	Whitlingham Junction	,,	3	48	49	
120	2	Salhouse	,,	3	55	12	
123	1	Wroxham	,,	3	58	21	35 m.p.h.
127	23	Worstead	,,	4	3	53	
130	11	North Walsham ..	arr.	4	8	0	
			dep.	4	12	2	
133	75	Gunton	pass.	4	17	50	30 m.p.h.
138	13	Cromer	arr.	4	24	5	

A schedule of a journey in July 1908 with Driver Cage in charge.

The "Norfolk Coast Express" was one of the Great Eastern's first fully-vestibuled, all-bogie trains, and when it replaced the "Cromer Express" in 1907 the train was a 12-vehicle formation consisting (from the Cromer end) of a brake third, two third class vehicles, an open third, a restaurant car, an open first, a compartment first, a full brake, a composite, a brake third, another composite, and finally a further brake third. The first eight coaches were the main Cromer portion, while the next two vehicles constituted the two-coach Sheringham section; the two rearmost vehicles were the Overstrand portion.

Although in theory the "Norfolk Coast Express" weighed 317 tons, a fully laden train, replete with Edwardian travellers and their copious luggage, was many tons heavier, and if (as sometimes happened at the height of the summer) extra vehicles were added to cope with additional passengers, the "Norfolk Coast Express" might weigh anything up to 400 tons; C.J. Allen has even suggested that, on one occasion, the up train consisted of seventeen coaches weighing "at least 460 tons".

Such loadings were clearly beyond the normal capacities of a single-wheeled locomotive, and by the early years of the present century the "Cromer Express" and its successor were headed by newly-built 'Claud Hamilton' 4–4–0s. The first 'Claud', No. 1900 *Claud Hamilton*, emerged from Stratford Works in 1900, and further engines were built in batches over the next few years. Perversely, the 'Clauds' were numbered backwards from 1900 to 1789, the final batch (Nos. 1789–80) being delivered after the grouping.[34]

The new 4–4–0s had 7 ft coupled wheels and 19 in. x 26 in. inside cylinders. They carried the Great Eastern's distinctive dark blue livery, and this attractive colour scheme was further enhanced by the provision of brass-capped chimneys, brass-rimmed splashers and burnished steel smoke box door rings. The 'Clauds' were destined for a very long association with the Cromer branch, but in the Edwardian era they were perhaps best-known for their work on the "Norfolk Coast Express", and to Edwardian railway enthusiasts the 'Claud Hamilton' 4–4–0s were probably the Great Eastern express engines *par excellence*.

Although the "Norfolk Coast Express" was, without doubt, the most famous train on the Cromer branch, the heavily-loaded morning up and evening down restaurant car expresses were of more use to business travellers, who were able to save time on their long journeys to work by taking breakfast in the morning and dinner on the homeward-bound train in the evening.

Restaurant Car Services

Evidence of the relatively large numbers of people wishing to take their meals on GER trains can be seen in the succession of tea-time expresses that left Liverpool Street at roughly five minute intervals, taking long-distance commuters to Cromer, Hunstanton, Clacton or other East Anglian destinations. Significantly, these evening down trains were among the best services on the Great Eastern, and on the Cromer line, the 4.55 pm dining car train was probably the premier business express; in the up direction, the train left Cromer at 8 am, providing a useful connection to London throughout the year. (The "Norfolk Coast Express" was a summer-only working).

The role of comfortable, restaurant car services in stimulating long-distance commuter traffic should not be under estimated, and contemporary observers were well aware that the Great Eastern's policy "of providing liberally for the comfort" of business travellers had produced tangible results. In 1910, for example, *The Railway Magazine* printed the following assessment of GER restaurant car policies:

> This enterprising policy . . . has already been productive of distinctly encouraging financial results . . . the directors may, indeed, be said to have gone further than any other railway board, in that they have established not merely the breakfast, luncheon, tea and dining cars now familiar in even comparatively short-distance traffic, but also a supper car . . . every one of these services has from the beginning proved conspicuously successful, and there is little doubt that they are contributing in a material degree to the present prosperity of the railway. The restaurant cars are admirably designed, and the travelling kitchens, which form an essential part of the modern stock, are considered to be among the best in the country. They are, indeed, models of compact arrangement – embodying the essential features of those in ocean liners and in the best hotels – and the *chefs* are prepared to serve hot luncheon or dinner to as many as 130 first and third class passengers . . . Congratulations may well be offered to Mr H.C. Amendt, the manager of the Great Eastern Railway Hotels, who is principally responsible for the excellent results which have here been achieved. The new trains are vestibuled, and corridors throughout enable travellers to join the restaurant cars whenever they wish.

The train service provided during the Edwardian period consisted of about 12 passenger workings each way between Cromer and Norwich, with most services continuing through to London. As usual on GER lines, connections were given for both Liverpool Street and St Pancras – the latter station (reached via the Tottenham & Hampstead Joint line) being particularly convenient for people residing in Hampstead or other fashionable middle class areas.

The October 1908 public timetable shows a total of 11 up and 11 down trains, the best morning service being the 8 am from Cromer, which reached Liverpool Street at 11.25 am. The "Norfolk Coast Express", as such, did not run during the winter, but the 1.30 pm from Liverpool Street provided a somewhat slower substitute, with an arrival time in Cromer at 4.56 pm. The corresponding up service left Cromer at 1.13 pm, and arrived in London by 4.50 pm. It is interesting to note that travellers from Sheringham or Mundesley were also offered a range of through services or connections to London – although the timetables warned passengers on the 12.22 pm and 7.15 pm trains from Mundesley-on-Sea that they would have to "cross from the Mid. & GN Joint to the Great Eastern company's station at North Walsham" in order to continue their journeys!

By M&GN to Poppyland

The lure of "Poppyland" was such that Cromer attracted large numbers of summer visitors, not only from London but also from the East Midlands, and in this context it is worth considering the part played by the rival Midland &

Great Northern line in the development of this Norfolk resort. Unlike the Great Eastern, the M&GN was not well-placed to provide fast business expresses to and from London, and as far as Cromer was concerned the "Joint" was primarily a holiday line, carrying holidaymakers from the Midlands to Norfolk (and thereby establishing patterns of seaside holidaymaking that have persisted into the motor age).

Journeys on the M&GN invariably began far afield in distant provincial cities such as Nottingham or Leicester, from where through trains were hauled – sometimes by the Joint's own locomotives – to the "border" stations at Peterborough or Bourne. Passing from the metals of the parent companies, trains set off along single lines towards the holiday resorts of Sheringham, Cromer, Yarmouth or (via a line shared with the GER) Lowestoft.

The observant traveller would find much of interest; the engine, for instance, might be a Midland-style 4–4–0, similar to those on the Midland proper, but painted in the Joint's glorious "mustard yellow" livery. Other Midland types seen on the line included Johnson class 2, 0–6–0 goods engines, some of which were later rebuilt as class 3s. There were also some GN style Ivatt 0–6–0s, though the Midland had assumed overall control of the locomotive department in 1893.

Long distance cross country trains actually joined the M&GN at Little Bytham, but there was no station here and Bourne, 4 miles further on, was effectively the "start" of the Joint. Continuing eastwards, the M&GN main line ran via Spalding, where an avoiding line was opened in 1893 to bypass the GNR station. On, across the flat, monotonous expanse of south Lincolnshire, the single line continued, punctuated occasionally by little red brick stations such as Moulton (13¾ miles from Bourne) and Holbeach (17 miles).

Noticeable features of the line included its distinctive GN style somersault signals and standard Great Northern signal cabins. Many of these were equipped with Alfred Whitaker's patent tablet-exchanging apparatus, by means of which drivers could exchange single line tablets at speed; the metal "arms" which collected and received tablets from passing trains were situated in front of each signal cabin. Another noticable aspect of the M&GN was the very large number of level crossings, especially on the western sections of the route.

The Peterborough line converged from the right at Sutton Bridge (25¼ miles), and, after a pause in the station, trains crossed a combined rail and road bridge over the River Nene. The railway doubled immediately beyond, and entered the County of Norfolk. A long timber viaduct carried the line across the River Ouse at South Lynn (34¼ miles), after which M&GN trains crossed first the Great Eastern King Lynn route then, two miles further on the GER Dereham branch.

Heading north-east, the railway entered hillier, more interesting countryside, and became single once again after the wayside station at Grimston Road (40¾ miles). This section of the route had been opened as far as Massingham by the Lynn & Fakenham Railway on 16th August, 1879. The line became double at Raynham Park, and the up and down lines continued for the next 13½ miles to Melton Constable, the hub of the M&GN system.

Opened as a through station on the Lynn & Fakenham's Norwich extension on 2nd December, 1882, Melton became a junction following the opening of the "main line" to North Walsham on 5th April, 1883. When, in the following year, the initial section of the Cromer branch was opened to traffic, the station became a focal point with lines radiating north, south, east, and west! Passenger facilities were concentrated on a long island platform, reached by steps which descended from a road overbridge, "Great Central" fashion. The extensive station buildings included a refreshment room for the benefit of travellers waiting for Norwich or Cromer local services. To the south, a miniature locomotive works provided engineering back-up for the Joint's small fleet of locomotives. In 1904, a small 4–4–2T was actually built from scratch here, followed by two identical engines in 1909.

Many M&GN through trains conveyed portions for Lowestoft, Yarmouth and Cromer, and it was usual for these workings to go their separate ways from Melton Constable – from where Cromer portions would reverse direction in order to gain the M&GN Cromer branch.

With a fresh engine coupled at what had been the rear, Cromer portions continued north-eastwards towards the coast, and when the grey North Sea appeared on the left hand side, excited Edwardian children would know that they were at last nearing "Poppyland". At Sheringham (67¼ miles from Bourne) those with a knowledge of railways might have looked for GER vehicles in the bay platform – for the Great Eastern had running powers over the M&GN to this point. Onwards, the journey continued through increasingly-attractive coastal scenery until, at Cromer, the 71 mile journey ended beside the single platform of the M&GN's Cromer terminus (which was known as Cromer Beach to distinguish it from the nearby GER station – known simply as Cromer until the word "High" was appended in 1948).

From Cromer Beach, it was possible to continue, via the Norfolk & Suffolk Joint line, to Mundesley and thence to North Walsham, but the number of local services on this picturesque route was limited to about three M&GN trains each way. In general, most trains terminated at either Overstrand or Mundesley-on-Sea – from which point it was usually possible to find a GER connecting service to North Walsham. Additionally, the M&GN operated its own local service based on the southern end of the line, with trains running between North Walsham and Mundesley.

Excursion Traffic

Despite the inherent rivalry existing between Great Eastern and M&GN railwaymen, the two companies worked amicably on the Norfolk & Suffolk Joint Line (which was, in fact, *two* railways, with a detached southern section between Yarmouth and Lowestoft in addition to the coastal line from North Walsham to Cromer). These good working relations were possible because, in the Edwardian era at least, the GER and M&GN companies catered for two more or less distinct markets. As we have seen, the Great Eastern specialised in carrying well-off Londoners to and from North Norfolk, whereas the M&GN catered more for East Midlanders spending their holidays in East Anglia.

The vast majority of Cromer's summer guests or long-stay residents were all of middle or upper-middle class origins, and like other British seaside resorts, Cromer's humbler, working class patrons came as day trippers on special excursion trains. At a time of slowly-rising living standards, the Great Eastern and M&GN railways realised that there was a vast, untapped market in terms of working class leisure travel, and both organisations tried to stimulate demand by offering reasonably-priced excursion tickets from London or other centres of poulation.

It was, indeed, in the field of cheap day tickets, that the two railways were in active competition for Cromer traffic, and both the GER and M&GN offered attractively-priced excursions from London. On Sundays and on Bank holidays (i.e. when regular traffic was slack) it was usually possible to reach Cromer from either Liverpool Street or the Great Northern station at Kings Cross. In 1903, for example, the GNR advertised a day trip from Kings Cross to Yarmouth or Cromer for just 4 shillings return, while at around the same time the Great Eastern offered similarly-priced tickets to a whole range of coastal towns. These long excursions "of the Great Eastern to the North Sea coast", wrote W.J. Gordon in the late 1890s, afforded many examples of what "that rising company" could do; some were "cheap enough to recall the days of the the great competition, when the fare from Leeds to London was five shillings, and occasionally half a crown"![35]

In addition to its special cheap fare offers, the Great Northern provided a regular through carriage from Kings Cross to Cromer and Mundesley-on-Sea, with departures from London at 3 pm and return workings from Mundelsey at 11.45 am.

Edwardian Motive Power

With its excellent services of fast trains to and from London, the Cromer branch became, in the Edwardian period, an extension of the London to Norwich main line, and in addition to the 'Claud Hamilton' 4–4–0s which worked the "Norfolk Coast Express" and other important workings, 'T19' class 2–4–0s and other main line classes regularly appeared on the branch. The 'T19s' had first been introduced in 1886, and there were eventually no less than 110 of them, numbered in random batches from 700 to 779, 781 to 790 and from 1010 to 1039.[36] Designed for express passenger duties, they had 7 ft diameter coupled wheels and 18 in. x 24 in. inside cylinders. In 1902 the GER fitted some of the 'T19s' with large diameter boilers, in which form the resulting "fat-bodied" engines became known as "Humpty Dumpties"! In a later development, some of the class were given large boilers and leading bogies, and in this guise the 'T19s' eventually became better-known as LNER 'D13s'. Other 2–4–0 types seen on the Cromer branch at the turn-of-the-century were the famous "Intermediate" or 'T26' 2–4–0s, and the much older 'No. 1 class' 2–4–0s which remained at work in the Norwich area until about 1912. Holden's 'T26' class were mixed traffic engines with 5 ft diameter driving wheels and 17½ in. x 24 in. inside cylinders. One hundred of these attractive machines were built at Stratford Works between 1891 and 1902, and like the"'Claud Hamilton' 4–4–0s, they were destined for a very long life (the last one was withdrawn from service in 1959 and can now be seen in the National Railway Museum at York).

Equally famous were the Worsdell-designed 'Y14' class 0–6–0s, 289 of which were built between 1883 and 1913. Intended primarily for freight work, they were nevertheless pressed into service as passenger engines during the height of summer – when large volumes of additional traffic frequently placed a great strain on the operating department; the 'Y14s' had 4 ft 11 in. wheels and 17½ in. x 24 in. cylinders.

Bromley 'E10' tanks and other 0–4–4Ts continued to be used on the line, but Worsdell 'M15' 2–4–2Ts and the visually-similar Holden 2–4–2 tanks were also widely used at this time, and on 23rd July, 1906 'M15' No. 678 hauled the first train over the newly-opened Norfolk & Suffolk Joint line from Roughton Road Junction to Runton West Junction and thence to Sheringham.[37] First introduced in 1884, the 'M15' class remained in production under James Holden, and the last did not appear until 1911; the 'M15s' had 5 ft 4 in. coupled wheels and 18 in. x 24 in. inside cylinders. For fast main line work, Holden also built a class of 2–4–2 radial tanks with 5 ft 8 in. wheels, and these engines often hauled the Mundesley and Sheringham portions of the "Norfolk Coast Express" from North Walsham to the coast.

In exceptional circumstances, the "Norfolk Coast Express" was double-headed by two 'Claud Hamilton' 4–4–0s, but in 1912 the introduction of Holden's 'S69' (or '1500') class 4–6–0s provided the GER with an express locomotive equal to the most arduous summer-Saturday tasks. The 'S69s' were enlarged 'Claud Hamiltons' with 26 in. x 28 in. cylinders and much bigger boilers; their coupled wheels had a slightly reduced diameter of 6 ft 6 in. and this gave them an added advantage on the 1 in 80 gradients encountered on the line to Cromer. Visually, the new engines were similar to their 4–4–0 predecessors with the same capped chimneys and beaded splashers.

Unfortunately, one of these 4–6–0s was involved in a collision at Colchester while working the up "Norfolk Coast Express" in July 1913, and the engine involved (No. 1506) was so badly damaged that it was subsequently broken up.

World War One

On 4th August, 1914 the outbreak of World War I dealt a death-blow to the "Poppyland" era, and with Cromer very much in the front line of an expected German attack, the celebrated "Norfolk Coast Express" was withdrawn.

Norfolk coast resorts such as Cromer were intimately connected with the war by reason of their position on the East Coast. Not surprisingly, few people now felt like spending their holidays in East Anglia, and trains that had recently carried holidaymakers started to carry ever-increasing numbers of military personnel. There was widespread fear of an enemy landing, and on 3rd November, 1914 a squadron of German battlecruisers shelled a beach near Great Yarmouth with little effect. Other minor raids followed, but no large scale naval attack was every mounted; instead the enemy used their new weapons – the airships – to bomb Eastern England from the air.

With the war bogged down on the Western Front, the Germans launched further raids throughout 1916 and 1917, and on several occasions, local railways were used as navigational features by airship commanders. Perhaps surprisingly, the railways rarely became targets, although on one night in August 1916 Zeppelin L11 dropped an incendiary bomb at Wroxham.[38] In a subsequent raid, on the night of 2nd–3rd September, 1916, airships flew over North Walsham at least four times without releasing their bombs, while on 23rd September, 1916 a Zeppelin raider dropped a bomb in the sea off Cromer (presumably aimed at a ship).

It was soon realised that in the absence of sophisticated navigational aids, Zeppelin commanders were relying heavily on visual navigation, and by introducing a nightly "blackout", the raiders could easily be frustrated in their attempts to reach given targets. For this reason, blackout regulations were rushed into effect, and it is interesting to note that special measures were taken to shield railway signal lamps, so that airship crews would be unable to follow railway lines on moonless-nights. Railwaymen were also expected to keep a look-out for the nightly raiders, and when Zeppelins were spotted, the time of sighting was immediately telegraphed to London. With reports coming in from every station on the airship's flight path, it was possible to build-up a very clear picture of the enemy's movements, and this vital information was of immense use to defending aircraft – which could be sent up to intercept the vulnerable airships before they returned to their bases across the North Sea.

Air defence of the British Isles was carried out by the Royal Naval Air Service, and with East Anglia an obvious target for Zeppelin attack, the RNAS stationed many of its own airships or fixed-wing aircraft in Norfolk; there was, for example, a naval air station at Bacton (near Mundesley), together with a seaplane station on Hickling Broad (to the east of Wroxham). The army, too, was called upon to garrison coastal areas as a precaution against invasion or (more likely) hit-and-run raids such as the British themselves launched against Zeebrugge in 1918.

With so many soldiers and sailors in the area the Cromer line carried significant military traffic throughout the years of conflict; train services were reduced in both speed and frequency, but with so many officers stationed on the Norfolk coast, the GER continued to provide restaurant car facilities to and from Cromer (a facility enjoyed by few other seaside resorts at that time!) These dining facilities were available on the 10 am Liverpool Street to Cromer and on the 5.30 pm return working from Cromer to London.

Zeppelin raids continued on and off throughout the war, and on the night of 19th–20th October, 1917 three airships crossed the coast between Cromer and Wells intending, perhaps, to bomb London or some other urban centre. One of the raiders parted company with its companions near County School, and, having dropped at least three bombs between Dereham and Hardingham, it turned north east towards the coast.[39] Railway staff at Wroxham – having no doubt been warned by their colleagues at neighbouring GER stations – reported the Zeppelin overhead at about 10.40 pm, and five minutes later the raider dropped its last bomb on the blacked-out countryside (the commander was possibly hoping to hit the seaplanes on nearby Hickling Broad).

In the days before mechanised warfare, rail transport was expected to play an active part in the conduct of military operations, and in addition to using its sophisticated communications systems to report Zeppelin sightings, the Great Eastern was called upon to transport large numbers of troops. Secret plans, drawn up at the start of the war, had earmarked certain stations as military railheads to which troops would be despatched at short notice and, in anticipation of a more aggressive military role, the GER and M&GN systems were patrolled by a specially-constructed armoured train.

Built in the London & North Western workshops at Crewe, this unusual military train was one of a pair sent to threatened areas. It consisted of a Great Northern 0–6–2T, encased in half inch armoured steel plate; this heavily-protected locomotive was marshalled between two bogie infantry vehicles (adapted from Great Western Railway 40 ton loco coal wagons), and the train also featured gun-carrying vehicles, equipped with maxim guns and naval 12-pounders. The train could be driven from either end, or in conventional fashion from the locomotive, and it spent its life patrolling the Mundesley-on-Sea branch and other lines in the north Norfolk area.[40]

In general the Great War resulted in a reduction of ordinary services, but the Cromer branch retained a relatively "full" train service. One adverse result of the war was the abandonment of the Great Eastern's famous royal blue livery, and in its place GER engines were painted in drab, dark grey.

Local railways remained in a state of readiness until the early months of 1918, but as the conflict approached its end the anti-invasion precautions were scaled down; by August, it was clear that Germany was on the point of defeat, and on 11th November, 1918 the Great War was brought to a close.

The cost of ultimate victory had been appalling, not only in financial but also in human terms. For the first time in its history, Britain had tried to fight a land war (as opposed to a naval conflict) with the result that over a million men had lost their lives on the Western Front and elsewhere. No town or village had been spared, and the long lists of names on countless war memorials remain to this day as mute reminders of those who died for what they thought would be a better world.

Many local railwaymen had served in the army, among them S.S. Lee who, in civilian life, had been a goods porter at North Walsham, and John Sidney Neale who, before the war, had been a porter, also at North Walsham. S.S. Lee was killed on 29th April, 1918 while serving with the Norfolk Regiment, while his former colleague John Neale died in action on 27th September, 1918. Other casualties included Reginald Grimes (killed 1918), formerly a horse lad, and Ernest James Preston, a former booking clerk who was killed in Mesopotamia in October 1918; both men had worked at North Walsham – a station that seems to have lost an unusually-high number of its staff in the final year of the war.

With so many men serving in HM Forces, the railways were obliged to employ female staff in jobs that had hitherto been regarded as "mens work", and in this capacity at least two females were employed at Cromer. The ladies in question were Maud Watts and Catherine Woodehouse, who started work at the station in 1917. When they left after the cessation of the war, their male colleagues organised a presentation, and the occasion was fully reported by *The Great Eastern Railway Magazine* in February 1920:

> Presentations have recently been made by Mr T.H. Youell, station master, Cromer, to two of the female staff who joined the service in the early part of 1917 and have now relinquished their wartime work at the station. Miss Maud Watts, clerk, was the recipient of a gold-mounted fountain pen, and Miss Catherine Mabel Woodehouse, parcels cart driver, a leather weekend case. Mr Youell, in making the presentations, spoke in high terms of the way in which they had come forward to help the railway company, and indeed the country, at a time of great difficulty. Mr E. Chissell, booking clerk, also paid a tribute to their work, and hoped the small presents would be a reminder of the kindly feeling entertained for them by all the station staff.

A few months previously, the *GER Magazine* had reported a similar presentation that had been made to long-serving Wroxham station master Francis G. Underhill on the occasion of his retirement after 51 years service. The Magazine recalled that Mr Underhill's railway career had started as far back as 1866, when he commenced work at Dunham station (on the Norwich –Dereham line) where his own father was station master. Coming to Wroxham in 1879, station master Underhill remained at the station for no less than 38 years, in which time he became a familiar figure to successive generations of travellers. To mark his retirement, Mr Underhill was presented with a cheque for £140, "accompanied by many cordial expressions of appreciation and regard", but sadly, the former station master died a few months later at the relatively early age of sixty-seven.

The Last Years of the GER

The years of conflict against Imperial Germany had left all railways in a run-down condition, and their recovery was not helped by a coal strike in 1920/21, which disrupted railway services in many parts of the country. Fortunately, the Great Eastern – having abandoned oil firing when the price of oil fuel became uneconomic – had not scrapped all of its oil-burning equipment, and by burning a mixture of oil, wood and coal, the GER was able to provide a credible service at a time when other lines were badly-hit by the lack of adequate coal supplies. In May 1921 it was reported that "about 50 engines" had been fitted with oil-burning apparatus, and although the locomotives concerned were chiefly main line classes, the use of oil fuel enabled limited coal supplies to be consumed by branch and suburban engines. By this means, the Great Eastern was able to beat the strike, and from 30th May, 1921 the company was able to *increase* the emergency train service in time for the summer season.[41]

Holiday traffic built-up fairly rapidly in the months following World War I, but the war had produced great changes in British society, and whereas, before 1914, Cromer had been a residential town, it became purely a seaside resort in the changed conditions pertaining after 1918. This changing role reflected the declining status of a middle class that could no longer afford to pay servants, maintain two homes, or commute ultra-long distances to and from work and with fewer people wishing to use the railway to reach London, there was less incentive for the GER to provide large numbers of fast business expresses to and from distant resorts such as Cromer.

The 1922 timetable shows just 8 up and 8 down trains, though most of these trains apparently worked through to Liverpool Street. The best morning up service left Cromer at 7.46 am, and arrived in London by 11.22 am, while in the opposite direction afternoon expresses left Liverpool Street at 3.10 pm and 5.22 pm, arriving in Cromer at 6.53 pm and 9.24 pm respectively. All of these services conveyed restaurant cars – a facility provided also on the 1 pm up and 10 am down workings. An interesting feature of Cromer branch operation at this time was the provision of a limited number of through Pullman cars to London (*see chapter 4*). Significantly, no trains ran through to St Pancras, and the days when travellers from Cromer GER to London had the choice of two metropolitan terminals had gone for good.

The 1922 timetable was, in truth, a shadow of that provided prior to 1914–18, and although branch train services were still relatively good, times had clearly changed for the worse. An air of ineluctable decline hung over the railway, and this comparative deterioration was apparent in the engine colours which had changed from the well-known royal blue of pre-1914 days to a sombre dark grey livery of funereal aspect. (The GER coach livery had been changed to maroon shortly after the war.) With the "Grouping" of railways soon to take place, the Cromer branch was, in a sense, in a kind of limbo, and nobody could foretell what the uncertain future held in store for this popular seaside line.

Sources for Chapter 3

31 V.L. Whitechurch, Cromer, *The Railway Magazine*, June 1898 p.510.
32 C.J. Allen, The Norfolk Coast Express, *Railway World*, January 1967 pp. 20–23.
33 W.A. Tuplin, *British Steam Since 1900* (1969) p.24.
34 C.J. Allen, *The Great Eastern Railway* (1955) pp. 127–38.
35 W.J. Gordon, *Every-day Life on the Railroad* (1898)
36 E.L. Ahrons, Locomotive & Train Working in the Latter Part of the 19th century, *The Railway Magazine*, 1918 p.246.
37 *The Locomotive Magazine*, 1906.
38 Official reports held at the Fleet Air Arm Museum, RNAS Yeovilton.
39 *Ibid.*
40 G. Balfour, *The Armoured Train; its Development and Usage* (1981) *passim.*
41 *The Railway Magazine*, May 1921.

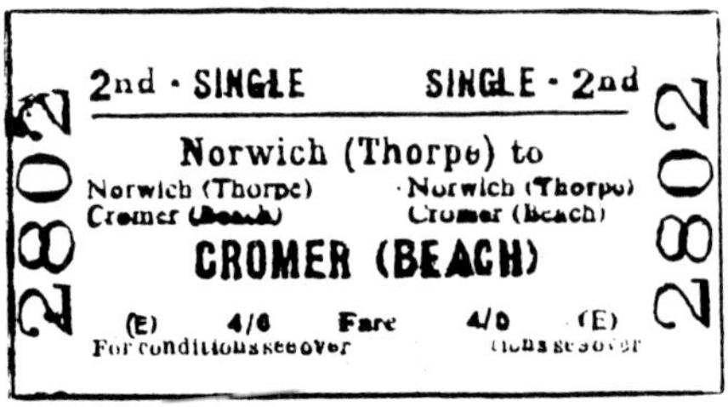

NORWICH, WROXHAM, NORTH WALSHAM, CROMER, MUNDESLEY, OVERSTRAND, AND SHERINGHAM.

See page	Station		WEEK DAYS morn	morn	morn	morn	morn	morn	even.	SO even.	even.	even.	even.	even.	even.	even.	SUNDAYS morn	morn	even.	even.
							Third Class Pullman Car London to Cromer.	Restaurant Cars London to Cromer.					Restaurant Cars London to Cromer.		Restaurant Cars London to Cromer.					
8 to 10	LONDON (Liverpool St.)	dep.	...	...	5 0	...	8 15	10 0	...	12 25	...	...	3 10	3 15	5 22	...	...	9 20	...	4 40
	Colchester	"	—	—	6 23	—	9 40	11 28	—	1 6	1 5	—	3 53	4 31	5 22	—	—	10 56	—	5 56
	Ipswich	"	...	...	6 56	...	10 9	11 57	12 4	2 5	2 14	...	4 46	5 0	7 0	...	...	11 34	...	6 38
	Norwich (Thorpe)	arr.	—	—	8 43	—	11 21	1 17	1 56	3 6	4 9	—	5 47	6 41	8 19	—	—	1 27	—	8 30
35 to 37	LONDON (Liverpool St.)	dep.	...	...	5 8	...	...	...	...	...	11 50	...	...	...	...	...	...	9 25	...	...
	Cambridge	"	—	—	6 39	—	B 8 12	10 6	—	—	1 24	—	—	4 15	—	—	—	11 25	—	5 0
	Ely	"	...	...	7 7	...	B 8 19	10 43	...	...	2 15	...	...	5 0	...	...	...	11 55	...	5 45
	Norwich (Thorpe)	arr.	—	—	8 56	—	B 10 39	12 25	—	—	4 6	—	—	6 49	—	—	—	1 45	—	7 30
	NORWICH (Thorpe)	dep.	6 19	7 5	9 21	9 43	11 26	1 23	2 4	3 11	4 31	4 47	5 54	6 52	8 24	8 32	10 9	2 9	6 51	9 9
	Whitlingham (for Thorpe St. Andrew)	"	6 26	7 12	9 31	9 50	—	—	2 11	—	4 38	4 54	—	7 0	—	8 39	10 16	2 16	6 58	9 16
	Salhouse	"	6 36	7 22	9 41	10 0	...	...	2 21	...	4 48	5 4	6 9	7 10	8 39	8 49	10 26	2 26	7 8	9 26
	Wroxham	"	6 41	7 28	9 48	10 5	11 43	1 41	2 26	3 31	4 55	5 9	6 16	7 17	8 46	8 54	10 33	2 33	7 15	9 33
	Worstead	"		7 37	9 57		11 52	1 50		...	5 4		—	7 26	8 55		10 42	2 42	7 24	9 42
	North Walsham	arr.	—	7 43	10 3	—	11 58	1 57	—	3 45	5 10	—	6 29	7 32	9 2	—	10 48	2 48	7 30	9 48
		dep.	...	7 45	10 5	...	12 1	1 59	...	3 48	5 12	...	6 32	7 34	9 4	...	10 50	2 50	7 32	9 50
	Gunton	"	—	7 56	10 13	—	12 9	2 7	—	3 56	5 21	—	6 41	7 41	9 12	—	10 58	2 58	7 40	9 58
	CROMER	arr.	...	8 8	10 25	...	12 21	2 19	...	4 8	5 31	...	6 53	7 54	9 24	...	11 8	3 8	7 50	10 8
62	North Walsham (G.E.)	dep.	—	8 6	10 27	—	12 9	2 5	—	3 55	—	—	5 37	—	9 10	—	October only.	—	October only.	October only.
	North Walsham (M. & G.N.)	arr.	...	...	...	...	...	...	...	...	...	...	...	...	...	...		...		
N. & S.C.	Paston and Knapton	"	—	8 15	10 37	—	12 18	2 14	—	4 4	—	—	6 46	—	9 19	—		—		
	Mundesley-on-Sea	"	...	8 19	10 42	...	12 22	2 18	...	4 8	...	...	6 50	...	9 23	...		...		
	Trimingham	"	—	8 27	10 59	—	12 41	2 26	—	4 17	—	—	6 58	—	—	—		—		
	OVERSTRAND	"	...	8 32	11 5	...	12 55	2 31	...	4 22	...	...	7 3	...	...	...		...		
	CROMER	dep.	—	—	—	—	—	—	—	—	5 40	—	—	—	—	—	—	—	—	—
	West Runton	arr.	...	8 18	10 35	...	12 41	2 29	...	4 18	5 56	...	7 9	...	9 34	...	...	...	...	...
	SHERINGHAM	"	—	8 22	10 39	—	12 45	2 33	—	4 22	6 0	—	7 13	—	9 38	—	—	—	—	—

B On Saturdays leaves Cambridge 9.10, Ely 9.33, and arrives Norwich 11.0 a.m.

NS Not Saturdays.

SO Saturdays only.

For service between County School, Aylsham and Wroxham see page 63.

The 1922 GER Passenger Timetable for the line.

SHERINGHAM, OVERSTRAND, MUNDESLEY, CROMER, NORTH WALSHAM, WROXHAM AND NORWICH.

See page	Stations		Week Days morn	morn	morn	morn	morn	even	even	even	even	even	even	SO even	even	even	Sundays morn	even	even	even
					Restaurant Cars Cromer to London.				Restaurant Cars Cromer to London.	Third Class Pullman Car Cromer to London.			Restaurant Cars Cromer to London.							
	SHERINGHAM	dep.	...	...	7 23	...	8 45	...	12 30	...	3 10	...	5 5	...	...	8 16	...	...	...	...
	West Runton	„	—	—	7 27	—	8 49	—	12 34	—	3 14	—	5 9	—	—	8 20	—	—	—	—
	CROMER	arr.	...	...	7 40	...	9 2	...	12 47	...	3 27	...	5 22	...	...	8 33	...	...	...	...
62	M. & G. N. Overstrand	dep.	...	...	...	...	8 53	...	11 35	...	2 50	...	5 9	...	...	8 25	October only.	October only.	...	October only.
	Trimingham	„	—	—	—	—	8 59	—	11 45	—	3 1	—	5 15	—	—	8 31			—	
	Mundesley-on-Sea	„	...	...	7 35	...	9 6	...	12 52	...	3 19	...	5 23	...	...	8 38			...	
	Paston and Knapton	„	—	—	7 39	—	9 10	—	12 56	—	3 29	—	5 27	—	—	8 42			—	
	North Walsham M. & G. N.	arr.	...	...	...	...	...	...	...	...	...	...	...	...	...	...			...	
	North Walsham G. E.	„	—	—	7 47	—	9 18	—	1 4	—	3 38	—	5 35	—	—	8 50			—	
	CROMER	dep.	6 30	...	7 46	...	9 10	...	1 0	2 22	3 33	...	5 30	7 33	...	8 46	8 50	1 0	4 50	8 0
	Gunton	„	6 39	—	7 55	—	9 19	—	—	2 31	3 42	—	5 39	7 43	—	8 55	8 59	1 9	5 0	8 9
	North Walsham	arr.	6 46	...	8 2	...	9 26	...	1 15	2 38	3 49	...	5 46	7 50	...	9 2	9 6	1 16	5 7	8 16
	North Walsham	dep.	6 48	—	8 4	—	9 29	—	1 20	2 40	3 51	—	5 49	7 52	—	9 4	9 7	1 17	5 10	8 18
	Worstead	„	6 54	...	8 10	...	9 36	...	...	2 46	3 57	...	5 55	7 58	...	9 10	9 13	1 23	5 17	8 24
	Wroxham	„	7 3	7 54	8 20	9 38	9 47	1 15	1 34	2 56	4 6	5 53	6 6	8 8	8 24	9 20	9 22	1 32	5 28	8 31
	Salhouse	„	7 10	8 1	...	...	9 54	1 22	...	3 4	4 13	...	6 13	8 15	8 31	9 27	9 29	1 39	5 35	8 41
	Whitlingham (for Thorpe St. Andrew)	„	—	—	—	—	10 3	1 31	—	—	4 22	—	6 22	8 21	8 40	9 36	9 39	1 48	5 44	8 50
	NORWICH (Thorpe)	arr.	7 22	8 13	8 36	9 54	10 9	1 37	1 50	3 16	4 28	6 9	6 28	8 30	8 46	9 42	9 44	1 54	5 50	8 56
38 to 40	**Norwich (Thorpe)**	dep.	7 30	—	8 44	—	10 30	—	1 55	4 21	4 59	—	7 39	—	—	10 24	9 54	2 24	6 5	10 21
	Ely	arr.	9 23	...	10 26	...	12 19	...	3 18	6 13	6 28	...	9 31	...	...	12 13	11 21	4 25	7 40	12 13
	Cambridge	„	9 56	—	11 4	—	12 52	—	3 47	—	7 1	—	10 4	—	—	12 45	...	5 0	8 14	12 45
	LONDON (Liverpool St.)	„	...	...	...	...	2 21	...	...	...	8 [illegible]	...	...	...	...	2 50 morn	...	6 40	9 40	3 0 morn
11 to 13	**Norwich (Thorpe)**	dep.	7 33 MO	—	8 41	—	10 22	—	2 7	3 23	4SO51	—	6 37	—	—	—	—	—	6 12	—
	Ipswich	arr.	8 51 MO	...	9 43	...	12 14	...	3 8	4 43	6SO25	...	7 49	...	...	...	...	...	8 9	...
	Colchester	„	9 24 MO	—	10 59	—	12 46	—	3 39	5 14	—	—	8 46	—	—	—	—	—	8 46	—
	LONDON (Liverpool St.)	„	10 39 MO	...	11 22	...	2 3	...	4 58	6 32	...	...	9 30	...	...	...	...	...	...	...

MO Mondays only. **SO** Saturdays only.

For service between County School, Aylsham and Wroxham see page 63.

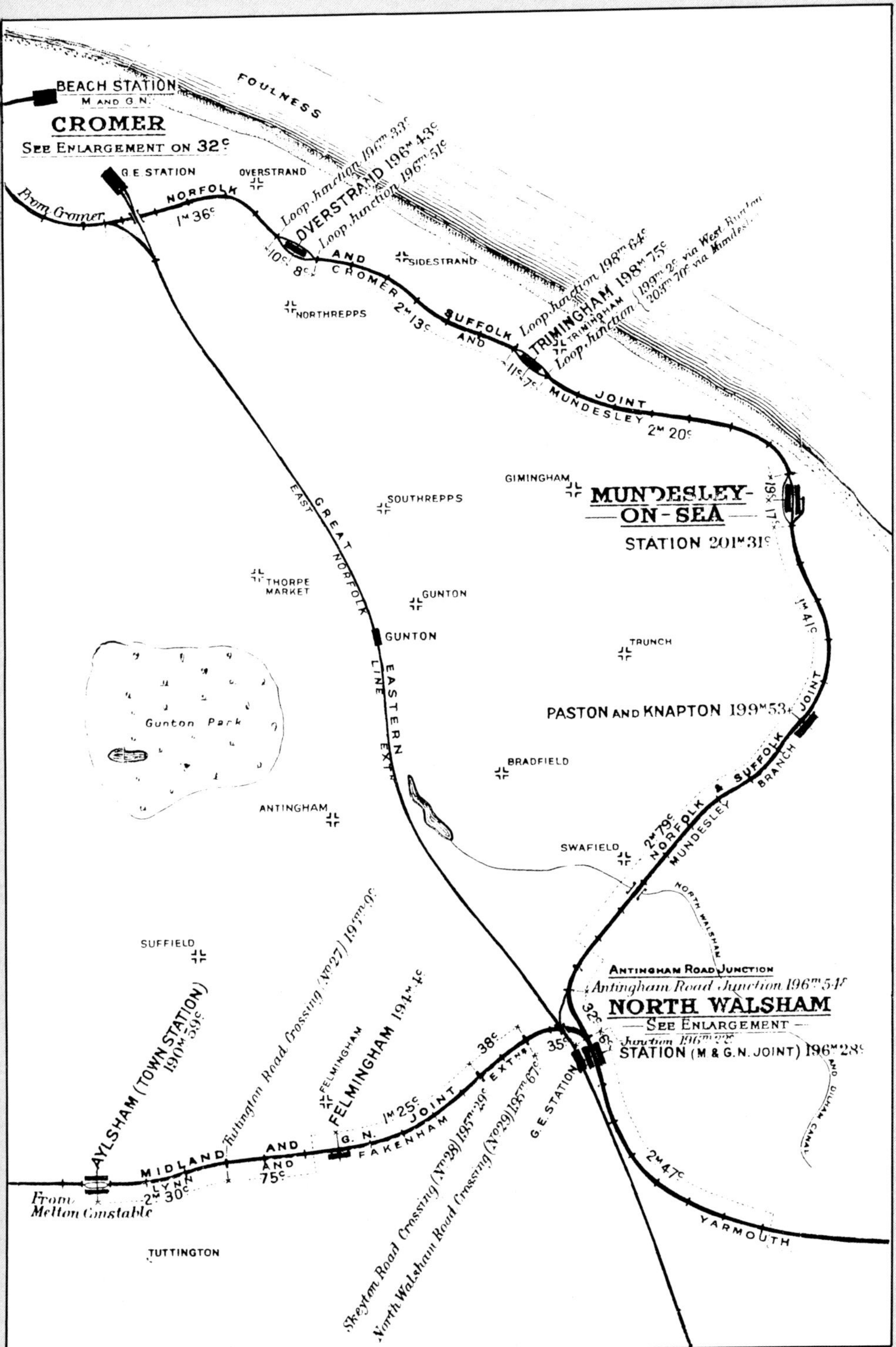

Extract from the 1921, Midland Railway Distance Diagram covering the GER and Mundesley Branch.

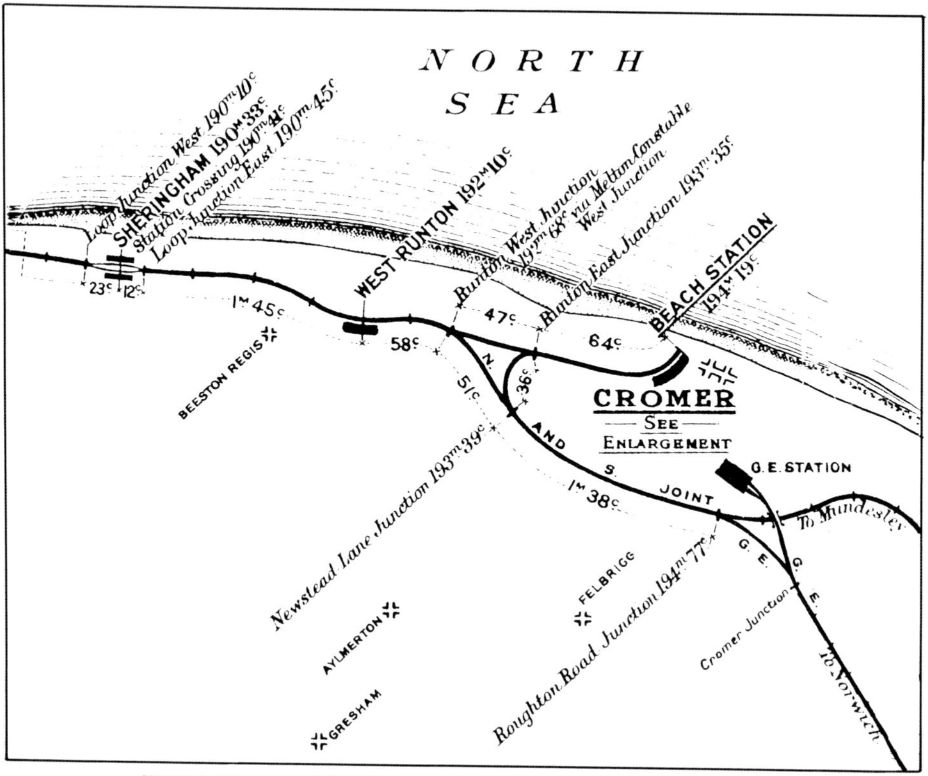

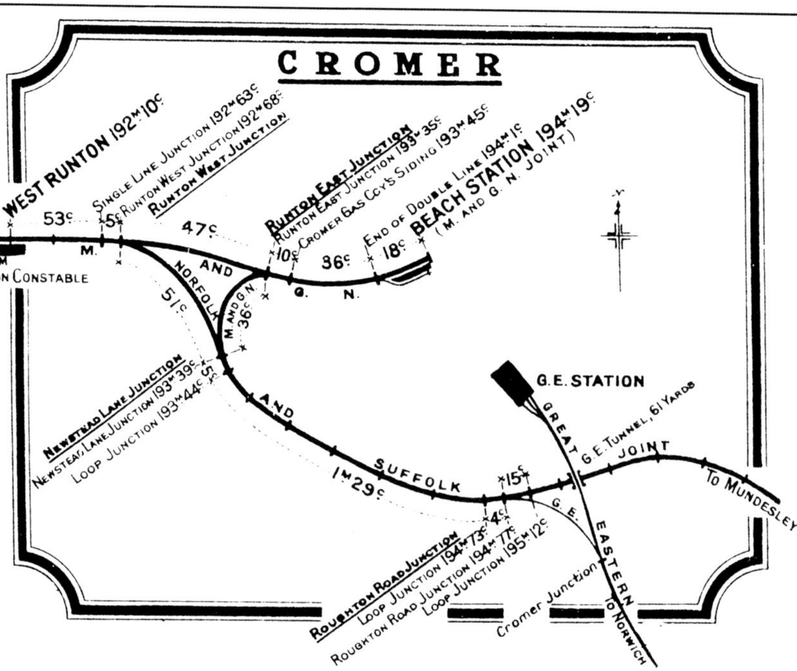

Enlargements of the Cromer and Sheringham areas from the Midland Railway Distance Diagram.

Chapter Four

The LNER Period (1923–1947)

On 1st January, 1923 the diverse railway companies that had, for so long, served the transport needs of Britain, were "grouped" into four major companies under the provisions of the Transport Act 1921. The GER, GNR, Great Central, North Eastern (and other companies) were amalgamated into a company known as the London & North Eastern Railway, but the situation regarding Cromer Beach and the M&GN was more complex in that its two owning companies were grouped into separate concerns – the Great Northern becoming part of the LNER whereas the Midland became an integral part of the London, Midland & Scottish group. This resulted in an anomalous situation in which, despite the grouping, the Midland and Great Northern Railway retained its separate existence as a jointly-owned LNER/LMS line.

Post Grouping Developments

In the short term, the 1923 grouping produced few obvious changes, and as in 1881, most ordinary travellers would have been unaware that a change of ownership had taken place. In the ensuing months, however, the newly-created LNER introduced its own, distinctive livery scheme – though Great Eastern men may have wondered if the decision to apply Great Northern-style apple green liveries to locomotives with driving wheels greater than 6ft 6in. was evidence of a certain bias towards the GNR. Similarly with passenger rolling stock, the LNER decided to standardise on a "varnished teak" livery resembling that favoured by the GNR and other constituents of the eastern group. This was in effect a reversion to the traditional GER colours, but it was, in practice, exceedingly difficult to remove paint from ex-GER coaches that had been painted maroon, and in consequence the "varnish teak" finish applied to former Great Eastern vehicles was usually brown paint. (Indeed, true varnished teak was found mainly on LNER main line stock, and large numbers of the company's ordinary vehicles received the above-mentioned overall brown livery.)

In visual terms, the new LNER apple green livery was much more attractive than the sombre dark grey that Great Eastern engines had carried since World War I, but sadly this colour scheme was not applied to smaller locomotives – which appeared in an uninteresting black livery.

Apart from these new liveries, the LNER initiated an entirely new system of class notation based upon engine wheelbases. This new system was both logical and simple, in that all large Pacific engines became 'A's, 4–6–0s received a 'B' prefix, Atlantics became 'C's, 4–4–0s were denoted by a 'D' prefix, and so on. As there was usually more than one type of engine with a particular wheelbase the basic notations were further sub-divided by the addition of numerals denoting each class. As far as Cromer services were concerned, the familiar 'Claud Hamilton' 4–4–0s became LNER classes 'D15', 'D16/2' or 'D16/3', while the rebuilt 'T19s' became LNER class 'D13' and the 'T26' 2–4–0s became LNER class 'E4'; Worsdell's 'Y14' 0–6–0s were designated class 'J15', and Holden's 5ft 8in. 2–4–2Ts became class 'F3'. These classes remained at work on the Cromer branch throughout the

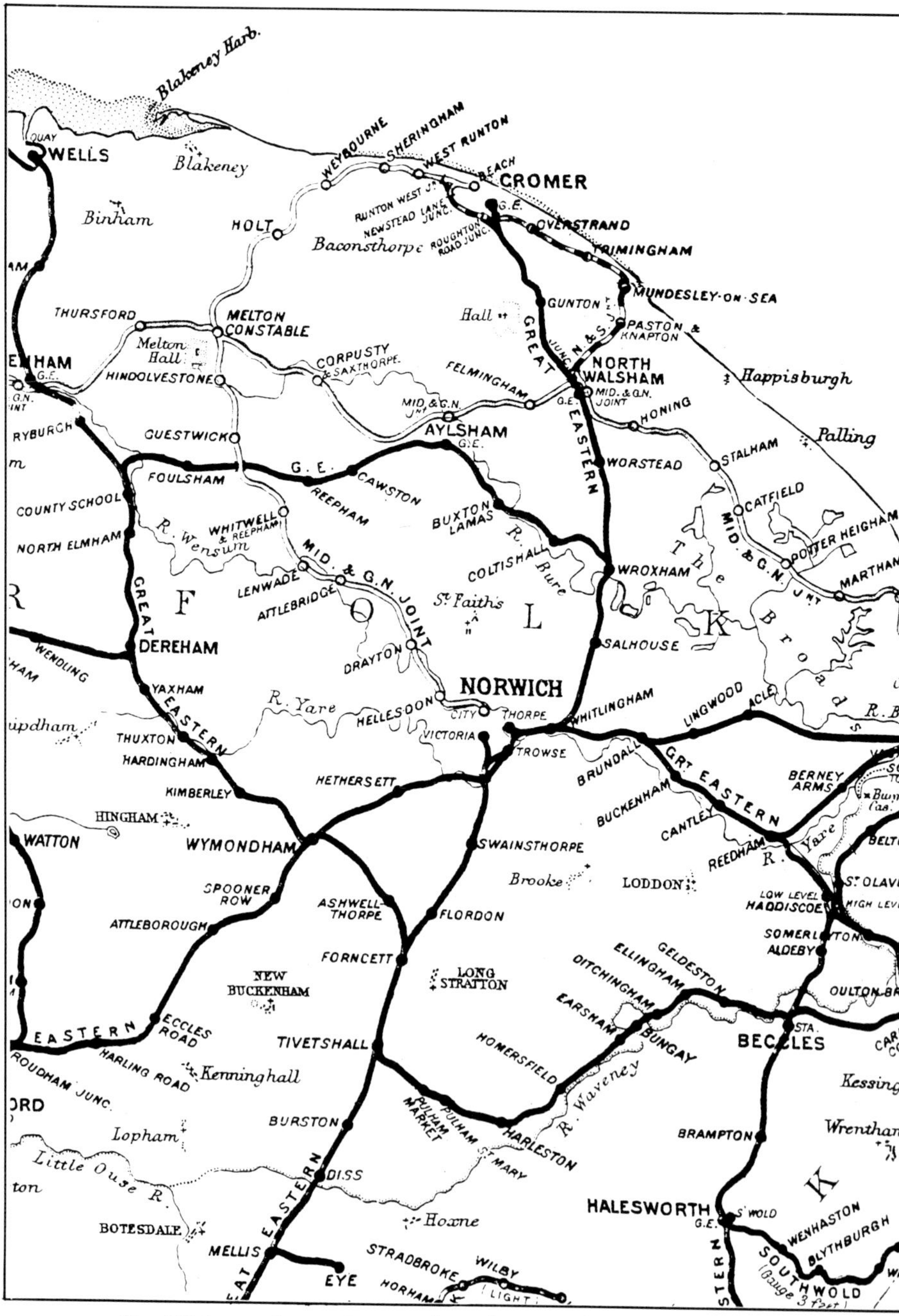

The RCH map of 1921 showing the railways in the North Norfolk area.

1920s and 1930s, together with a variety of other types including 'B12' 4–6–0s, 'J17' 0–6–0s, 'J19' 0–6–0s, 'B17' 0–6–0s, 'F4' 2–4–2Ts and 'F6' 2–4–2Ts.

Although the heyday of long-distance commuting came to an end in 1914–18, the post-war years were a time of growing leisure travel in which seaside resorts such as Cromer began to cater for increasing numbers of working class holidaymakers. Despite widespread unemployment, more and more British families began to take an annual, two-week summer holiday, and in these circumstances Cromer emerged as a popular resort among those seeking quiet, relaxing holidays amidst attractive coastal scenery. The LNER did much to encourage holiday travel, and each year the company published attractive posters, guide books and other promotional literature, extolling the virtues of Cromer, Sheringham, Mundesley and other resorts.

Railway publicity material often reached high standards in terms of content and artistic design, and there was immense rivalry between the "big four" companies. The Great Western usually won this annual "contest", but the London & North Eastern often came a close second; in 1931, for example, LNER holiday publicity featured a map of the entire East Coast from Essex to Lossiemouth, linked to a diagramatic Barometer which indicated "Very Dry"; the caption was "LNER for the *Drier Side*". Having thus suggested (quite rightly) that East Coast resorts were drier than the Great Western's rival Atlantic coast resorts, the LNER publicity department later went one better and turned the indented coastline of eastern England into a gigantic Yale key. An ingenious headline proclaimed that the LNER was "the key to a tonic holiday" on the East Coast – "The Drier Side".

Mundesley Branch Rationalisation

Such beguiling publicity did much to increase the popularity of Cromer and other East Coast resorts, but Sidestrand, Mundesley, and Overstrand stubbornly refused to develop as large scale resorts, and the lavish facilities provided on the Norfolk & Suffolk coast line never handled appreciable numbers of holidaymakers. In truth, the coast line had become an expensive "white elephant" in relation to the small numbers of people wishing to use its over-large stations, and the 1920s and 1930s were, in consequence, a time of rationalisation in which the line was reduced to local status by a progressive reduction in facilities. At Overstrand and Trimingham, for example, the signal boxes were taken out of use as early as the 1920s, and thereafter the line was worked on just two block sections between Roughton Road Junction and Mundesley, and from Mundesley to North Walsham. Sidings remained *in situ* at both stations, but in an attempt to reduce expenditure booking office staff were withdrawn and intending passengers had to buy their tickets from conductor guards. A similar situation pertained at Paston & Knapton, and by 1930 Mundesley-on-Sea was the only full-staffed and signalled station on the branch.[42]

To facilitate "conductor guard" operation, the branch train service was operated with the aid of former main line corridor coaches, and G.T. Moody, who travelled on the line in 1923, recalled that the coaches used at that time were ex-GNR corridor six-wheelers from which the lavatory fittings had been removed.

Pullman Cars on the Cromer Branch

Although the untimely withdrawal of the "Norfolk Coast Express" from Cromer to London was a blow to Cromer's prestige as a fashionable holiday town, there was compensation in the 1930s when the LNER initiated its famous "Eastern Belle" Pullman excursions to Cromer and other East Coast resorts. Pullmans had first appeared on the Cromer line in the early 1920s following the introduction of a small fleet of ten Pullman cars for use on the "Hook Continental" express and other East Anglian services. Built by Claytons of Lincoln, these GER Pullmans included five first class cars which, in typical Pullman fashion, were named *Arcadia*, *Ansonia*, *Cambria*, *Catania* and *Corsair*.

By 1922, Pullman services had been extended to Cromer and at least one Pullman car was included in the formation of the 8.15 am Liverpool Street to Cromer and the 2.22 pm return working. In the event, these East Anglian Pullman services failed to attract sufficient custom, and they were withdrawn after a few months trial operation. C.J. Allen has suggested that East Anglians did not take kindly to the payment of supplementary fares, and this is a plausible explanation when one recalls that the area had once been a stronghold of Puritanism; one can imagine the response of a non-conformist tradesman when asked to spend an extra few shillings simply to ride in a named car! On the other hand, the fact remains that before World War I, Norfolk-based commuters had paid extra to travel up to London in a conspicuously-luxurious fashion, and had Pullman services been available at that time they might have been successful. In the changed conditions after World War I, however, the number of high class, long distance commuters was declining, and faced with a dearth of such customers the LNER withdrew its East Anglian Pullmans and concentrated instead on the successful Harwich route and on entirely new, long distance Pullman services on the East Coast Main Line.

Expansion to Sheffield and Manchester was less successful, and by the mid-1920s the company owned an embarrassingly-large number of expensive Pullman cars for use on a limited number of viable routes. It was, perhaps, to find use for these otherwise redundant vehicles that in June 1929 the LNER introduced its celebrated "Eastern Belle" Summer Pullman trips.[43] These ran to a varied programme, taking excursionists to a range of holiday resorts throughout East Anglia. The programme varied from season to season, but a typical week invariably began with a Sunday trip to Clacton. Clacton – a popular destination – would be served again in mid-week, while on Mondays, Tuesdays, Thursdays and Fridays the train might visit Cromer, Felixstowe, Aldeburgh, Harwich, Hunstanton, or other East Coast resorts. In addition to these main destinations, various intermedidate resorts were also served; a Cromer service might also serve Wroxham, for example, while Harwich trips would call at Dovercourt Bay. In 1930, no less than 18 different resorts were covered throughout the season, and Cromer was visited, on average, once every week.

The 1934 "Eastern Belle" programme provided some of the fastest timings ever attempted in regular service on the Great Eastern system, and on the days when the train ran to Cromer, Sheringham or Yarmouth the booked time from Liverpool Street to Ipswich was only 79 minutes for the intervening 68.7 miles (i.e. some six minutes faster than normal timings on the Colchester main line). Cromer itself was reached in just 2 hours 58 minutes inclusive of intermediate stops at Wroxham and North Walsham – timings which recalled the great days of the "Norfolk Coast Express" and its 2 hour 55 minute schedules.

The "Eastern Belle" ran every day except Saturdays (when it would have duplicated regular holiday trains) and the train usually ran non-stop to its first destination. A typical week's running, in 1934, was as follows:

Sunday	Clacton (1 hour 30 minutes)
Monday	Wroxham, North Walsham and Cromer (2 hours 58 minutes)
Tuesday	Thorpeness and Aldeburgh (1 hour 30 minutes)
Wednesday	Clacton (1 hour 30 minutes)
Thursday	Wroxham, West Runton and Sheringham (3 hours 30 minutes)
Friday	Skegness (3 hours 25 minutes)

The train's formation varied, but there were typically seven or eight cars, one of which would be for first class travellers. The rest of the train was composed of third class vehicles, and this underlines a significant point; the "Eastern Belle" was designed, not for high class patrons but for average family groups. To this end its fares were commendably cheap, and for 16*s*. 6*d*. one could ride first class from London to Clacton inclusive of the Pullman supplement! The corresponding third class fare was 10*s*. on Sundays, but during the week these fares were reduced to just 10*s*. 6*d*. first class and 6*s*. 6*d*. third class for Essex or Suffolk resorts. More distant destinations such as Cromer or Sheringham cost 12*s*. 6*d*. first class and 7*s*. 6*d*. third class for the return journey.[44] In all, the "Eastern Belle" was a remarkable success, and the sight of chocolate and cream Pullman cars added a touch of glamour to the Cromer branch and other lines during the 1930s. Motive power on Cromer trips was usually a 'B12' 4–6–0.

Train Services in the 1920s and 1930s

Although the 2 hour 58 minute schedules of the "Eastern Belle" were obviously a highlight of the pre-war summer timetables, ordinary services had also improved in terms of frequency during the 1920s and 1930s, and by 1938 the basic train service between Cromer and Norwich consisted of 13 up and 14 down workings. The service was augmented during the summer months, when extra trains ran on Saturdays and also Sundays. Many trains continued through to London, and in the down direction, the 9.48 am, 12.33, 3.40 and 5.16 pm departures from Liverpool Street to Cromer conveyed restaurant cars, while in the opposite direction the 8.57 am from Cromer provided a restaurant car service to Norwich, and the 8.00 am and

5.30 pm departures conveyed restaurant cars through to Liverpool Street. An interesting innovation was the introduction, in 1934, of a special summer Saturdays "Holiday Camps Express" between Liverpool Street, North Walsham and Caistor-on-Sea.

In October 1936 the LNER assumed full responsibility for the Midland & Northern system, and this important development led to a greater integration of services on the hitherto separate M&GN and GER systems. The loop lines linking Cromer Beach and the GER station did not permit through running between the two stations, but some trains ran from Melton Constable to Cromer Beach and thence (after reversal) to Norwich and Liverpool Street. The 1938 summer timetable provided a through restaurant car train from Sheringham to Liverpool Street, which left Sheringham at 12.20 pm and ran direct to North Walsham without calling at Cromer.

In spite of the rationalisation of facilities at Overstrand and Trimingham, the Mundesley line gained two new stopping places in the 1920s and 1930s; both were simple halts, and the first, at Cromer Links was opened to the public in 1923. Situated between Overstrand and Roughton Road Junctiion, this new halt was intended to serve golfers at the nearby Royal Cromer Golf Club. A second halt, serving the coastal settlement of Sidestrand, was opened on 25th May, 1936 in the hope that tourists would be encouraged to visit the very heart of Clement Scott's "Poppyland". For walkers, the halt provided a useful starting point for a variety of clifftop rambles, but in retrospect Sidestrand should perhaps have been opened in the Edwardian era when "Poppyland" and "The Garden of Sleep" would clearly have attracted large numbers of excursionists. By 1936 the "Poppyland" era was already over, and it is doubtful if many visitors would have been familiar with the area's literary associations.

There were, in general, around half a dozen trains each way between North Walsham, Mundesley and Cromer. In the 1930s, for instance, the basic service consisted of 6 up and 6 down trains with a limited number of short distance workings between North Walsham and Mundesley. There were also some services between Mundesley and Cromer Beach and (unusually) an unadvertised empty stock working from Overstrand to Cromer (GE), which reversed at Roughton Road Junction in order to enter the former Great Eastern terminus via Cromer Junction. The branch train was, around 1923, worked by a Midland and Great Northern 4–4–0T, though some North Walsham to Mundesley locals were composed of former Great Eastern locomotives and rolling stock.[45] Most trains used the Great Eastern station at North Walsham, while at Cromer the track layout dictated that all passenger trains used the M&GN station at Cromer Beach (there being no convenient route to and from Cromer GE).

An innovation, in 1925, was the introduction of a through train from Cromer Beach to Yarmouth which left Cromer at 9.35 am and reached Yarmouth Beach at 11.06 am, having travelled via Overstrand, Mundesley-on-Sea, North Walsham and the M&GN main line. The return working left Yarmouth at 5.15 pm, but as these timings did not permit Yarmouth-based holidaymakers to spend a day at Cromer, the M&GN later introduced a summer-only morning train from Yarmouth to Cromer Beach. Leaving Yarmouth at 10.50 am, this new service enabled holidaymakers to spend "5½ hours in Poppyland", and although the train initially ran on Tuesdays, Wednesdays and Thursdays only, there was sufficient traffic to justify daily workings (Saturdays excepted) from 1933 until 1939.

A further innovation came in 1935 when the M&GN arranged a through Mundesley-on-Sea to Birmingham service; leaving North Walsham at 8.38 am, the train travelled via Mundesley and Overstrand to Cromer – from where it departed on the main leg of its journey to Birmingham at 9.40 am. This useful through working was, however, poorly advertised, and there was no balancing down service for returning travellers.

The LNER takeover in 1936 did not lead to any changes in terms of operation, and the post-1936 timetable was generally similar to that provided by the Norfolk & Suffolk Joint committee. There were still half a dozen trains each way between Cromer Beach, Mundesley and North Walsham, while Sunday services consisted of a limited through service between Norwich Thorpe, Mundesley and Sheringham.

Locomotives seen on the Mundesley-on-Sea line in the later 1930s were similar to those employed on the Cromer "main line", and (although precise details are elusive) it would probably be true to say that ex-GER 2–4–2Ts were the type most widely used. Engines known to have worked on the line include 'F3' 2–4–2Ts Nos. 8089 and 8097, but 'F4', 'F5' and 'F6' locomotives are also likely to have been used at various times. Goods traffic was probably worked by 'J15' 0–6–0s, while excursions from the former M&GN line occasionally brought more exotic types onto the branch – on one occasion an ex-Great Central Pollet single was noted heading an excursion train to Mundesley-on-Sea.

World War Two

On 3rd September, 1939 the people of Britain heard on their "wireless" sets that Herr Hitler had rejected Britain's ultimatum to cease hostilities in Poland, and that, in consequence Britain was at war with Germany. Many listeners expected the skies to fill with Luftwaffe bombers within the first few days, but in the event the initial months of the war were strangely quiet. For railway travellers, a reduction in services and the sight of servicemen hurrying to join their ships and units were reminders that there was a "war on".

A nightly blackout was put into effect, and to stop travellers from falling from the edges of darkened platforms a broad white line was hastily applied along each platform edge. In the slightly unreal conditions of "The Phoney War" curious and often humorous rumours began to gain credence, and there was much talk of "Fifth Columnists" who had supposedly been parachuted into Britain disguised as birdwatchers, monks, nuns and other unlikely characters!

The Fall of France in June 1940 dispelled any illusions about the gravity of the situation, and fearing imminent invasion the government ordered that all road signs and station nameboards should be taken down. Obstructions were placed in fields and open spaces to impede airborne landings, and able-bodied males were encouraged to join the Local Defence Volunteers (renamed the Home Guard in July 1940). The war had, in effect, entered a "Napoleonic" phase in which Britain stood alone against an armed and largely hostile Europe. In June 1940 an area extending from Sussex to the Wash was declared "unsafe", and thus – as in 1914 – Cromer, Mundesley and Sheringham found themselves in the "front line". Leisure trips were discouraged, and travellers were confronted with large notices asking them if their journeys were "really necessary"?

Elaborate defensive preparations were set up by September 1940 and if any German units had landed, they would have been met by regular troops stationed in the area, by Home Guard volunteers and (if the invaders managed to secure a bridgehead) by elite Home Guard "Special Units", who had been secretly trained to operate behind enemy lines.[46] Consisting mainly of poachers, gamekeepers and other men used to operating under cover of darkness, these 5,000 men had made elaborate plans, and although details are *still* secret, there can be little doubt that coastal railways such as the Cromer branch would themselves have been sabotaged as soon as they fell into enemy hands.

Bombing of civilian targets commenced with a mass raid on London's docklands on Saturday 7th September, 1940, and at 8.07 am, the codeword "Cromwell" was sent out from London in the mistaken belief that an invasion of the British Isles was imminent. At Cromer, naval personnel were ordered to man defensive positions – and it is said that an over-enthusiastic explosive officer was, with difficulty, prevented from blowing up the town's pier!

In common with other seaside routes, the Cromer line was patrolled regularly by an armoured train from June 1940 until the Spring of 1943. Designed to alleviate Britain's acute shortage of armoured vehicles after the losses at Dunkirk, these units consisted of ex-GER 'F4' or 'F5' 2–4–2Ts, flanked by two personnel vehicles and two gun wagons. The trains were encased in ¼ inch steel plating, and armed with rifles, machine guns and naval-type six pounders which could be trained fore and aft; they carried crews of twenty-six including gunners, locomen, one officer, one NCO and a wireless operator.

There were, in all, a grand total of twelve such trains (together with several "spares") and each unit was given a distinguishing letter of the alphabet; the train based in North Norfolk was "Train G", and this unit regularly patrolled an area extending from Yarmouth to Kings Lynn; its locomotive was armoured 'F4' No. 7189.[47]

In June 1941 the Germans turned their attention towards Russia, and the first, critical phase of the war came to an end. Britain's military build-up nevertheless continued, with a heavy concentration of supply dumps, army camps and aerodromes scattered throughout East Anglia and other parts of southern Britain. These wartime establishments brought much extra traffic to the Cromer branch, and although holiday traffic had been extinguished by the war, the line remained busy carrying large numbers of soldiers and airmen.

In common with other railways, the Cromer, Mundesley and Sheringham lines suffered a cut in services at the start of the war, but as the war effort got into its stride extra trains were introduced to cater for service traffic. In 1942, for instance, the LNER provided a special, Saturday night train from Norwich to Cromer (via Mundesley) in order that locally-based servicemen could spend their off-duty evenings in Norwich. Inevitably, these late night trains were invariably packed with high-spirited revellers – some of them in an inebriated condition! They also carried representatives from most of the allied powers – there were, for instance, large numbers of Polish airmen in north-east Norfolk, in addition to British and Commonwealth forces.

Two of the largest establishments in the area were RAF Coltishall and RAF Rackheath, both of which were situated to the west of the Cromer branch – Rackheath being within easy walking distance of Salhouse station. Coltishall, which could be reached from either Wroxham or Worstead stations (or from Horstead on the Wroxham–County School branch) was an important military aerodrome, and by June 1944, it was operating a variety of high-performance aircraft including Spitfires of 504 Squadron and Mosquitos of 25 Squadron, together with Mustangs of 316 (Polish) Squadron.

The presence of such important targets as RAF Coltishall ensured that the north Norfolk area was frequently targeted by the Luftwaffe, but despite destructive raids on both Norwich and Cromer, the Cromer branch emerged from the war unscathed (Ryburgh, on the neighbouring Wells branch was less fortunate, and suffered a direct hit in August 1941 as a result of which its station buildings were destroyed).

The end of the war in Europe was followed by the election of Mr Attlee's Labour government, pledged to nationalise the railways and other important industries. The final months of private ownership were, in many ways, as traumatic as the war years, and with rationing and "austerity" still very much in force, Britain shivered through the worst winter in living memory in the early part of 1947. Train services had been severely disrupted and tragically, on 5th February, 1947, a permanent way man was run down by a train while trying to keep the Mundesley line free from snow drifts.

Sources for Chapter 4

42 E.Tuddenham, The Norfolk & Suffolk Joint, *Railway World* July 1966 pp. 288–92

43 *The Railway Magazine*, July 1929

44 Letter from G.T. Moody, *The Railway Magazine*, July 1972 p. 380

45 Letter from G.T. Moody, *Railway World*, November 1966 p. 486

46 David Lampe, *The Last Ditch* (1968) *passim.*

47 G. Balfour, *The Armoured Train; its Development & Usage* (1981) *passim.*

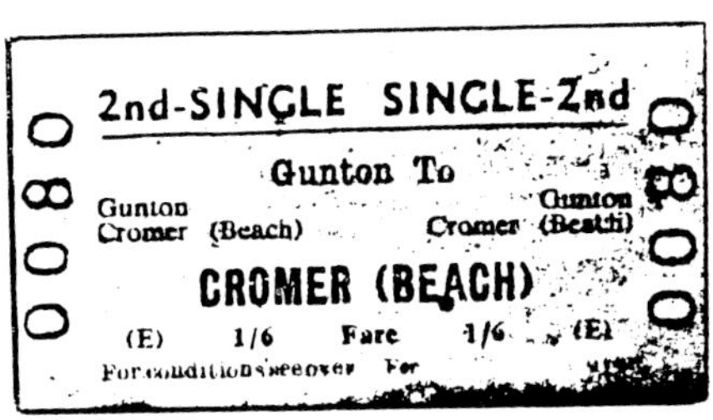

Table 46— *continued* SHERINGHAM, CROMER, MUNDESLEY-ON-SEA, NORTH WALSHAM, WROXHAM and NORWICH (Thorpe)

Miles from Cromer		Week Days															
		am A R THE BROADSMAN	am	am V R	am	am A R	am Sats. only. Runs 30th June to 8th Sept. incl	am F		am K	pm H HOLIDAY CAMPS EXPRESS Saturdays only	am A Saturdays only Commences 30th June		pm V Saturdays only	pm V Except Saturdays	pm Z Saturdays only. Runs 7th July to 1st September inclusive	pm M
	Sheringham .. .. dep	6 23	..	7 40	8X 4	8 20		9 23	..	10 9		11 23	..	12 5	12 26	..	1 23
	West Runton	6 27	....	7 44	8X 8	8 24		9 27	....	10 13		11 27	....	12 9	12 30	....	1 27
	Cromer (Beach) .. arr	6 32	..	7 49	8X13	8 29		9 32	..	10 18		11 32	..	12 14	12 35	..	1 32
—	Cromer (Beach) ..... dep	6 39	7 24	7 54	8X20	8 36		9 39	....	10 25		11 39	....	12 34	12 43	....	1 39
6¾	Gunton	6 54	7 39	..	8X41	8 54		9 54	..	10 40		..	..	12 51	12 58	..	1 54
10¾	North Walsham (M'n)arr	7 0	7 45	8 13	8X47	9 0		10 0	....	10 46		11 59	....	12 57	1 4	....	2 0
—	47 Mundesley-on-Sea..dep	6†41	7†23	7†55	..	8†30		9† 9	..	10†27		..	..	12†26	12†45	1 30	1C30
—	North Walsham (M'n)dp	7 2	7 46	8 14	....	9 2		10 2	....	10 47	....	12 3	....	12 59	1 6	1 48	2 2
13¾	Worstead	7 8	7 52	..	..	9 8		10 8	..	10 53	..	..	..	1 5	1 12	..	2 8
18	Wroxham	7 16	8 0	8 26	....	9 17	9 55	1017	....	11 1	12 9	12 18	....	1 14	1 20	2 4	2 16
20¾	Salhouse	7 24	8 8	..	..	9 25	10 3	1025	..	11 9	..	..	..	1 22	1 28	..	2 24
26¾	Norwich (Thorpe) .. arr	7 35	8 19	8 41	....	9 36	1014	1036	....	11 20	....	12 33	....	1 33	1 39	....	2 35
141¾	5 London (L'pool St) 6 ar	10 0	..	11 t18		12h35	..	1g35	..	1L 55	3 27	3 30	..	4 41	4 34	4 56	4P56

	Week Days—*continued*								Sundays										
	pm	pm R	pm B THE NORFOLKMAN	pm	pm K	pm K	pm J ② Saturdays only		pm Runs 1st July to 9th Sept. incl.	pm D Runs on 17th, 24th June and 16th September only	pm D Runs 1st July to 9th Sept. incl.		pm J ②	pm D	pm Runs 1st July to 9th Sept. incl.	pm Runs 24th June to 9th Sept. incl.	pm ②	pm	
Sheringham .. .. dep	2 57	..	4 26	5 23	6 29	8 43		..	..	1 6	1 16	..	..	5 0	..	7 0	..	..	..
West Runton	3 1	....	4 30	5 27	6 33	8 47		....	....	1 10	1 20	....	....	5 4	....	7 4	....	....	....
Cromer (Beach) .. arr	3 6	..	4 35	5 32	6 38	8 52		..	..	1 15	1 25	..	..	5 9	..	7 9	..	..	..
Cromer (Beach) ..... dep	....	3 39	4 42	5 39	6 48	9 0		....	12 34	1 22	1 32	....	....	5 16	5 51	7 16	....	8 38	....
Gunton	..	3 54	..	5 57	7 4	9 15		..	12 49	1 37	..	..	..	5 31	6 7	7 31	..	8 53	..
North Walsham (M'n)arr	....	4 0	5 3	6 3	7 10	9 21		....	12 55	1 43	1 52	....	....	5 37	6 12	7 37	....	8 59	....
47 Mundesley-on-Sea.. dep	..	..	4†35	5†30	6†51	9† 0	1028	..	12†34	1†24	1†24	..	5 6	..	..	7†19	..	..	..
North Walsham (M'n)dp	....	4 2	5 5	6 4	7 11	9 22	1040	....	12 56	1 45	1 53	....	5 18	5 39	6 14	7 38	8 1	9 0	....
Worstead	..	4 8	..	6 10	7 17	9 28	1047	..	1 2	1 51	..	..	5 25	5 45	6 20	7 44	8 8	9 6	..
Wroxham	....	4 16	5 20	6 19	7 25	9 36	1055	....	1 11	2 0	2 6	....	5 33	5 54	6 29	7 52	8 16	9 15	....
Salhouse	..	4 24	..	..	7 33	9 44	11 1	..	1 19	2 8	..	..	5 39	6 2	6 37	8 0	8 22	9 23	..
Norwich (Thorpe) .. arr	....	4 36	5 35	6 34	7 44	9 55	1112	....	1 30	2 21	2 21	....	5 50	6 13	6 48	8 11	8 33	9 34	....
5 London (L'pool St) 6 ar	..	7 45	7n55	9 12	..	2a23	..	..	..	5 20	5 20	..	9b 6	9 6	12a14	..	..	2a18	..

② or † Second class only
A Through Carriages between Sheringham and Liverpool Street
a am
B Refreshment Car between Sheringham and Liverpool Street
b First and Second class
C Saturdays only. Second class only until 30th June and on 8th and 15th September
D Through Train Holt to Liverpool Street (Table 51)
E Except Saturdays
F On Saturdays Through Carriages Sheringham to Liverpool Street
g Second class only between Norwich and Ipswich. On Saturdays arrives Liverpool Street 1 21 pm. First and Second class
H Through Train between Caister-on-Sea and Liverpool Street (Table 50). Light refreshments obtainable
h Arr 12 45 pm on Saturdays
J Through Train Mundesley-on-Sea to Norwich
K Through Carriages between Melton Constable and Norwich (Table 51)
L The East Anglian. Limited accommodation. Arr 2 6 pm on Fridays and Saturdays
M On Saturdays 30th June to 8th Sept. inclusive Through Carriages Sheringham and Refreshment Car Cromer to Liverpool Street
n On Saturdays arr 8 6 pm
P On Saturdays arr 5 6 pm
R Refreshment Car between Cromer and Liverpool Street
t On Mondays to Fridays until 22nd June and from 10th September arr 11 22 am
V Through Carriages between Melton Constable and Liverpool Street (Table 51)
X Except Saturdays. Does not run during School Holiday periods. For dates, see Supplement to Time Table
Z Through Train Mundesley-on-Sea to Liverpool Street

For OTHER TRAINS between Sheringham and Cromer, see Table 51

Table 47— *continued* MUNDESLEY-ON-SEA and NORTH WALSHAM (Main)

Second Class only except where otherwise shown

Miles		Week Days																					
		am		am		am		am		am		am		pm S		pm E		pm A	pm C		pm		pm
—	Mundesley-on-Sea * dep	6 41	....	7 23	....	7 55	....	8 30	....	9 9	....	1027	....	1226	....	1245	....	1 30	1 30	....	4 35	....	5 30
1¾	Paston and Knapton *	6 45	..	7 27	..	7 59	..	8 34	..	9 13	..	1031	..	1230	..	1249	..	1 36	1 34	..	4 39	..	5 34
5¼	Nth Walsham (Main) arr	6 52	....	7 34	....	8 6	....	8 41	....	9 20	....	1038	....	1237	....	1256	....	1 44	1 41	....	4 46	....	5 41

	Week Days—*continued*												Sundays										
	pm		pm		pm		pm		pm		pm P		pm		pm		pm		pm N		pm		
Mundesley-on-Sea * dep	6 14	....	6 51	....	8 15	....	9 0	....	9 49	....	1028	....	1234	..	1 24	....	2 57	....	5 6	....	7 19	..	....
Paston and Knapton *	6 18	..	6 55	..	8 19	..	9 4	..	9 53	..	1032	..	1238	....	1 28	..	3 1	..	5 10	..	7 23	....	..
Nth Walsham (Main) arr	6 25	....	7 2	....	8 26	....	9 11	....	10 0	....	1039	....	1245	..	1 35	....	3 8	....	5 17	....	7 30	..	....

* Tickets are issued on the train

A Saturdays only. Runs 7th July to 1st September inclusive. Through Train to Liverpool Street. First and Second class (Tables 46 and 5)
C Saturdays only. Runs until 30th June and on 8th and 15th September
E Except Saturdays
N Through Train to Norwich (Thorpe) (Table 46)
P On Saturdays Through Train to Norwich (Thorpe) arr 11 12 pm (Table 46)
S Saturdays only

The British Railways 1956 Timetable for the lines to Cromer and Mundesley-on-Sea.

Table 46 NORWICH (Thorpe), WROXHAM, NORTH WALSHAM, MUNDESLEY-ON-SEA, CROMER and SHERINGHAM

Week Days

Miles		pm	am		am	am (Saturdays only. Commences 30th June)	am	am K		am (Except Saturdays. Runs 25th June to 7th September inclusive)	am A R (Saturdays only. Runs 30th June to 8th September inclusive)	am B (THE NORFOLKMAN Except Saturdays)		am B (THE NORFOLKMAN Saturdays only)	pm (Saturdays only. Runs 30th June to 1st September inclusive)	pm	am J (Saturdays only)
	5 London (L'pool St.) 6 dp	10c30	..	..	..		..	4 35	..	5 54	8 30	9 30	..	9 30	..	..	9Y47
—	**Norwich** (Thorpe) .. dep	6a15	....	....	7 52		....	9 26	....	1026	11 22	11 53	....	11 59	1226	....	1252
6	Salhouse	6 29	..	..	8 6		..	9 40	..	1040	11 36	..	..	..	1240	..	..
8¾	**Wroxham**	6 36	....	....	8 12		....	9 47	....	1047	11 44	12 10	....	12 20	1246	....	1 9
13	Worstead	6 46	..	..	8 21		..	9 56	..	1056	11 53	..	..	..	1255	..	..
16	**North Walsham** (M'n) arr	6 53	....	....	8 28		....	10 3	....	11 3	12 0	12 22	....	12 35	1 2	....	1 21
21½	47 Mundesley-on-Sea .. arr	7†18	..	..	9† 1		..	10†22	..	..	12†21	12†40	..	12D54	..	..	..
—	**North Walsham** (M'n) dp	7 2	....	....	8 30		....	10 6	....	11 5	12 2	12 24	....	12 38	1 3	....	1 23
19¾	Gunton.	7 9	..	..	8 38		..	10 13	..	1112	12 9	12 33	..	..	1 10	..	..
26¾	**Cromer** (Beach) .... arr	7 23	....	....	8 52		....	10 27	....	1126	12 23	12 47	....	1 4	1 24	....	1 43
—	**Cromer** (Beach) .. dep	..	7 50	..	..	9 28	9 42	10 34	..	1134	12 30	12 56	..	1 11	..	1 35	1 50
28¾	West Runton	....	7 56	....	....	9 34	9 48	10 40	....	1140	12 36	1 2	....	1 17	....	1 41	1 56
30½	**Sheringham** .. .. arr	..	7 59	..	..	9 37	9 51	10 44	..	1144	12 40	1 6	..	1 21	..	1 44	2 0

Week Days—continued

	am R (Saturdays only)	pm (Saturdays only)	am R (Except Saturdays)	pm (Except Saturdays)	am H (HOLIDAY CAMPS EXPRESS Saturdays only)	pm V R	pm U (2) (Except Saturdays)	pm	pm A R	pm K		pm A R (THE BROADSMAN Except Saturdays)	pm A R (THE BROADSMAN Saturdays only)		pm	pm V	pm Q	pm (Saturdays only)
5 London (L'pool St.) 6 dp	1030	..	1030	..	1050	1230	..	..	1 30	..	..	3 30	3 30	..	..	5 30	6N30	7 30
Norwich (Thorpe) .. dep	1 19		1 35		....	3 2	3 42	....	4 42	5 18	....	5 42	6 0	....	6 33	8 5	9 29	1048
Salhouse	1 33		1 49		..	..	..	..	4 56	..	..	5 56	..	..	6 47	..	9 43	11 2
Wroxham	1 42		1 56		2 10	3 22	....	....	5 3	5 34	....	6 3	6 16	....	6 53	8 22	9 49	11 8
Worstead	1 51		2 5			..	..	..	5 12	..	..	6 12	..	..	7 2	..	9 58	1117
North Walsham (M'n) arr	1 58		2 12			3 37	4 8	....	5 19	5 46	....	6 19	6 28	....	7 9	8 34	10 5	1124
47 Mundesley-on-Sea .. arr	..		..			4d20	4 20	..	..	6† 7	..	6†46	6†46	..	7†33	8†52	10†22	..
North Walsham (M'n) dp	2 2		2 14			3 40		4X17	5 21	5 47	....	6 21	6 30	....	7 12	8 36	10 6	1125
Gunton.	2 11		2 23			3 55		4X24	5 28	5 56	..	6 30	6 39	..	7 19	..	10 13	1132
Cromer (Beach) .... arr	2 25		2 37			4 9		4X38	5 42	6 10	....	6 44	6 53	....	7 33	8 56	10 27	1146
Cromer (Beach) .. dep	..	2 29	..	3 5	..	4 15		4X45	5 49	6 17	..	6 51	7 0	..	..	9 3	10 34	..
West Runton	....	2 35	....	3 11	....	4 21		4X51	5 55	6 23	....	6 57	7 6	....	....	9 9	10 40	....
Sheringham .. .. arr	..	2 38	..	3 14	..	4 25		4X54	5 59	6 27	..	7 1	7 10	..	..	9 13	10 44	..

Sundays

	am T		am U (2)		am T (Runs 24th June to 9th Sept. incl)		am		pm U (2)		pm
5 London (L'pool St.) 6 dp	..	..	..	..	10 0	..	1030	..	2b24	..	2 24
Norwich (Thorpe) .. dep	10 0	....	1023	....	1 23	....	2 40	....	6 20	....	7 10
Salhouse	1014	..	1035	..	..	..	2 54	..	6 32	..	7 24
Wroxham	1020	....	1042	....	1 40	....	3 0	....	6 38	....	7 30
Worstead	1032	..	1051	..	1 49	..	3 9	..	6 47	..	7 39
North Walsham (M'n) arr	1039	....	1057	....	1 56	....	3 16	....	6 53	....	7 46
47 Mundesley-on-Sea .. arr	..	..	11 9	..	2†13	..	3†36	..	7 5	..	..
North Walsham (M'n) dp	1041	....	....	....	1 57	....	3 18	....	....	....	7 48
Gunton	1048	..	..	..	..	..	3 25	..	..	..	7 55
Cromer (Beach) .... arr	11 2	....	....	....	2 17	....	3 39	....	....	....	8 9
Cromer (Beach) .. dep	11 9	..	..	..	2 24	..	3 46	..	..	..	8 16
West Runton	1115	....	....	....	2 30	....	3 52	....	....	....	8 22
Sheringham .. .. arr	1119	..	..	..	2 34	..	3 56	..	..	..	8 26

(2) or † Second class only
A Through Carriages between Liverpool Street and Sheringham
a am
B Refreshment Car between Liverpool Street and Sheringham
b First and Second class
c On Sundays dep 11 30 pm
D Second class only until 30th June and on 8th and 15th September
d Second class only. On Saturdays arr 3 57 pm
H Through Train between Liverpool Street and Caister-on-Sea (Table 50) Light Refreshments obtainable
J From 23rd June to 1st September Through Carriages Liverpool Street to Sheringham
K Through Carriages between Norwich and Melton Constable (Table 51)
N The East Anglian. Limited accommodation
Q On Mondays, Fridays and Saturdays Through Train Norwich to Melton Constable (Table 51)
R Refreshment Car between Liverpool Street and Cromer
T Through Train Norwich to Holt (Table 51)
U Through Train to Mundesley-on-Sea
V Through Carriages between Liverpool Street and Melton Constable (Table 51)
X Except Saturdays. Does not run during School Holiday periods. For dates see Supplement to Time Tables
Y Saturdays only. Runs 23rd June to 1st September inclusive

For OTHER TRAINS between Cromer and Sheringham, see Table 51

Table 47 NORTH WALSHAM (Main) and MUNDESLEY-ON-SEA

Second class only except where otherwise shown

Week Days

Miles		am		am		am		am		am		pm S		pm E		pm A		pm S		pm C		pm
—	**Nth Walsham** (Main) dep	7 7	..	7 39	..	8 14	..	8 50	..	1011	..	1210	..	1229	....	1243	..	3 46	..	4 9	..	4 55
3½	Paston and Knapton *	7 14	....	7 46	....	8 21	....	8 57	....	1018	....	1217	....	1236	..	1250	....	3 53	....	4 16	....	5 2
5½	**Mundesley-on-Sea** .. arr	7 18	..	7 50	..	8 25	..	9 1	..	1022	..	1221	..	1240	....	1254	..	3 57	..	4 20	..	5 6

Week Days—continued / **Sundays**

	pm		pm		pm		pm		pm		pm		Sundays am N		pm		pm		pm		pm N		
Nth Walsham (Main) dep	5 56	..	6 35	..	7 22	..	8 41	..	9 28	..	1011	..	1058	..	1 0	..	2 2	..	3 25	..	6 54	..	..
Paston and Knapton *	6 3	....	6 42	....	7 29	....	8 48	....	9 35	....	1018	....	11 5	....	1 7	....	2 9	....	3 32	....	7 1	....	....
Mundesley-on-Sea .. arr	6 7	..	6 46	..	7 33	..	8 52	..	9 39	..	1022	..	11 9	..	1 11	..	2 13	..	3 36	..	7 5	..	..

* Tickets are issued on the train

A Saturdays only. Second class only until 30th June and on 8th and 15th September
C Except Saturdays. Through Train from Norwich (Thorpe)
E Except Saturdays
N Through Train from Norwich (Thorpe) (Table 46)
S Saturdays only

Class 'B1', 4–6–0, No. 61044 pulls into Wroxham station with the down 'Broadsman' express on the 12th May, 1953. *P.J. Kelly*

Class 'B12/3', No. 61568 on the 5.20 pm ex Cromer train, approaching Wroxham station on the 12th May, 1953. *P.J. Kelly*

Chapter Five

The British Railways Period (1948–1987)

At midnight on 31st December, 1947, a nationwide fanfare of locomotive whistles heralded the demise of private ownership and the creation of a new, national transport undertaking encompassing rail, road and water transport. In many places, a feeling of elation filled the air, and some railwaymen even chalked "they're ours now!" on the sides of wagons. In the short term, however, the immediate results of nationalisation were remarkably few, and the former London & North Eastern Railway was painlessly transformed into British Railways Eastern and North Eastern Regions.

The one obvious sign that a momentous change of ownership had in fact taken place concerned the liveries of locomotives and rolling stock. The varnished teak coach livery of the LNER was replaced by a novel, red and cream colour scheme which did much to brighten the rundown appearance of post-war Britain, while non-corridor coaches were painted in an overall maroon livery that was, in effect, a reversion to the short-lived GER red livery of the early 1900s. Locomotives, meanwhile, were painted in a range of liveries including lined LNWR-style black for "mixed traffic" locomotives such as 'B12' 4–6–0s, and plain, unadorned black for humbler goods classes such as 'J15' 0–6–0s.

Apart from livery changes, the one innovation initiated by BR locally was a logical renaming of Cromer station, which henceforth became "Cromer High" to distinguish it from the former M&GN terminus at Cromer Beach; in a simultaneous renaming, North Walsham was designated "North Walsham Main", while the M&GN station next door became "North Walsham Town". Explaining these renamings in a letter sent to local authorities, the Railway Executive claimed that it would "simplify matters for the public" if towns served by two or more stations were given stations with "distinctive names".

These changes were, in retrospect, merely cosmetic, and with few families having access to a car, the Cromer branch and other holiday lines were soon carrying pre-war levels of summer traffic as people flocked to the seaside in increasing numbers in the years following World War II.

Early Rationalisation

The early 1950s were, nevertheless, a time of modest rationalisation, and in September 1952 the former East Norfolk branch from Wroxham to County School lost its passenger service. In the following year, the Norfolk & Suffolk Joint line from Roughton Road Junction to Mundesley-on-Sea was closed to all traffic, the last trains running on Monday, 6th April, on which day Cromer Links Halt, Overstrand, Sidestrand Halt and Trimingham were deleted from the railway network. Ironically, the section of line involved in this closure had been one of the last to open; on the other hand, the demise of the Cromer to Mundesley line made sound economic sense because this coastal route – though highly picturesque – carried little traffic.

Further retraction came in September 1954 when the ex-Great Eastern station at Cromer High was closed to passenger traffic. Again, this was a long overdue piece of rationalisation for, as we have seen, Cromer High was inconveniently situated on the outskirts of the town. Norwich to Cromer passenger trains were henceforth routed into the former Midland & Great Northern terminus at Cromer Beach, and the ex-GER line from Cromer Junction to Cromer High station became a goods-only spur. Cromer Beach thereby became Cromer's main BR station, and for a few years the terminus handled both M&GN and East Norfolk line trains; the additional traffic was accommodated in what was, in effect, a single platform branch station with just one short bay – although the situation was improved somewhat by a platform extension and improved signalling.[48]

Train Services in the 1950s

Despite these early closures, the Cromer branch remained a busy holiday route throughout the 1950s, and its importance was underlined by the reappearance of named trains after World War II. In 1948, the "Norfolkman" express commenced running between London, Norwich and Cromer, and in 1950 the "Norfolkman" was joined by the "Broadsman"; with the reintroduction of the Saturdays-only "Holiday Camps Express" as a named working, the Cromer branch carried no less than three named expresses!

The "Norfolkman" originally left Liverpool Street at 10 am, but its departure time was later brought forward to 9.30 am. The train was allowed 2 hours 20 minutes for the 115 mile journey to Norwich Thorpe, although this time was subsequently cut to 2 hours 10 minutes. The "Broadsman", which left Liverpool Street at 3.30 pm, was also allowed a 2 hour 10 minute schedule in each direction between London and Norwich, but in September 1952 its timings were cut to just two hours in each direction – the first mile-a-minute schedule on the former Great Eastern system. Both trains called at intermediate stations north of Norwich, and until 1953 they also conveyed portions for Mundesley-on-Sea and Sheringham which travelled via the coastal route to Roughton Road Junction.

The 1956 public timetables provide a glimpse of a holiday line working at full capacity to move large numbers of travellers to and from the seaside. The basic weekly service provided 14 trains each way daily between Norwich Thorpe and Cromer Beach, together with several short-distance workings between Cromer and North Walsham. The Mundesley-on-Sea branch enjoyed a relatively frequent push-pull service of 14 up and 16 down workings to and from the GER station at North Walsham (Main), while the Cromer Beach to Melton Constable line was worked by a complex service of local and cross country trains – some of which worked through to Leicester or Birmingham via the M&GN "main line".

The popular "Norfolkman" and "Broadsman" expresses ran daily, with departures from Liverpool Street at 9.30 am and 3.30 pm respectively; the down "Norfolkman" reached Cromer Beach at 12.47 pm (1.04 pm on Saturdays) while the "Broadsman" followed some six hours later, and arrived in Cromer at 6.44 pm (6.53 pm on Saturdays). Both trains continued through to Sheringham (after reversal), the "Norfolkman" arriving at 1.06 pm while the "Broadsman" arrived at 7.01 pm. In the opposite direction the up "Norfolkman" left Sheringham at 4.26 pm, reaching Cromer Beach at 4.35 pm and

THE BROADSMAN

SHERINGHAM, CROMER, NORWICH, IPSWICH AND LONDON (Liverpool Street)

WEEKDAYS

Station		am
Sheringham	..dep	6 23
West Runton	"	6 27
Cromer (Beach)	"	6 39
Gunton	"	6 54
North Walsham (Main)	"	7 2
Worstead	"	7 8
Wroxham	"	7 16
Salhouse	"	7 24
Norwich (Thorpe)	"	7 45
Diss	"	8 11
Stowmarket	"	8 29
Ipswich	..arr	8 42
"	..dep	8 45
London (Liverpool St.)	..arr	10 0

Station		E pm	S pm
London (Liverpool St.)	..dep	3 30	3 30
Ipswich	..arr	4 43	4 53
"	..dep	4 46	4 56
Norwich (Thorpe)	..arr	5 30	5 51
Salhouse	"	5 56	..
Wroxham	"	6 3	6 16
Worstead	"	6 12	..
North Walsham (Main)	"	6 19	6 28
Gunton	"	6 30	6 39
Cromer (Beach)	"	6 44	6 53
West Runton	"	6 57	7 6
Sheringham	"	7 1	7 10

E Except Saturdays. **S** Saturdays only.

Refreshment Car available between Cromer (Beach) and London (Liverpool Street).

Passengers travelling from London (Liverpool Street), Sheringham and Cromer (Beach), and also from Norwich (Thorpe) to Ipswich and London (Liverpool Street) by this service can reserve seats in advance on payment of a fee of 1s. 0d. per seat.

THE NORFOLKMAN

LONDON (Liverpool Street), IPSWICH, NORWICH, CROMER and SHERINGHAM

WEEKDAYS

Station		E am	S am
London (Liverpool St.)	.dep	9 30	9 30
Ipswich	..arr	10 46	10 53
"	..dep	10 49	10 56
Norwich (Thorpe)	..arr	11 40	11 51
Wroxham	"	12 10	12 20
North Walsham (Main)	"	12 22	12 35
Gunton	"	12 33	..
Cromer (Beach)	"	12 47	1 4
West Runton	"	1 2	1 17
Sheringham	"	1 6	1 21

Station		E pm	S pm
Sheringham	..dep	4 26	4 26
West Runton	"	4 30	4 30
Cromer (Beach)	"	4 42	4 42
North Walsham (Main)	"	5 5	5 5
Wroxham	"	5 20	5 20
Norwich (Thorpe)	"	5 45	5 45
Ipswich	..arr	6 36	6 38
"	..dep	6 38	6 41
London (Liverpool St.)	..arr	7 55	8 6

E—Except Saturdays.

S—Saturdays only.

Refreshment Car available between London (Liverpool Street) and Sheringham.

Passengers travelling from London (Liverpool Street), Sheringham and Cromer (Beach), and also from Norwich (Thorpe) to Ipswich and London (Liverpool Street), by th. service can reserve seats in advance on payment of a fee of 1s. 0d. per seat.

Details of just two of the expresses serving Cromer in 1956.

London by 7.55 pm. The "Broadsman", meanwhile, remained in Norfolk overnight in order to form an early morning departure from Sheringham to Liverpool Street at 6.23 am on the following day.

In addition to the "Norfolkman" and "Broadsman" expresses which ran every day except Sundays, the Saturdays Only "Holiday Camps Express" left Liverpool Street at 10.50 am and called at Wroxham at 2.10 pm before continuing on its circuitous journey to Caister-on-Sea via North Walsham and the M&GN line. This train, which had run every summer Saturday since 1934 (with an unavoidable interruption in 1939–45), was, in many ways, a unique service. Its route was, to say the least, unusual in that it travelled via Cambridge, Thetford and the Wensum Curve at Norwich, and having reached North Walsham the train drew forward onto the Mundesley-on-Sea branch as far as Antingham Junction. The train engine (usually a 'B1' 4–6–0) was then detached while a Standard class '4MT' was coupled to what had been the rear for the remainder of the journey to Potter Heigham, Hemsby, Caister Camp Halt and Caister-on-Sea. In the up direction, a corresponding working left Caister-on-Sea at 10.41 am, and after reversing once again at Antingham Junction the train returned to London calling *en route* at Wroxham at 12.09 pm.

Sunday services were provided on a comparatively lavish scale during the early British Railways era, and in June 1956 local travellers had a choice of 8 up and 6 down trains on the lower part of the branch between Norwich and North Walsham. Most of these services were through workings from Holt or Mundesley-on-Sea to Liverpool Street, and in the down direction, the return workings continued through to either Holt, Sheringham or Mundesley; those wishing to travel between Mundesley and North Walsham could choose from 5 up and 5 down trains, including the above-mentioned through services to Norwich Thorpe.

Steam and Diesel Motive Power

In locomotive terms, the former East Norfolk route was still worked by 'Claud Hamilton' 4–4–0s and other veteran Great Eastern loco classes. Longer distance local services from Cromer to Norwich were typically worked by 'D15', 'D16/2' or 'D16/3' 4–4–0s, while Cromer to North Walsham locals were usually hauled by 'F3' or 'F6' 2–4–2Ts or other tank classes; for a time, the Mundesley to North Walsham push-pull service was worked by an 'N7' 0–6–2T.[49]

Engines used on the Cromer branch at this time were based at Norwich or at Melton Constable, with a small allocation at Cromer Beach. Until 1954 the ex-GER shed at Cromer High had also been used, but when that station lost its passenger services the remaining locomotives were transferred to the M&GN shed. In 1950, the local sheds housed large numbers of 'Claud Hamiltons', including Nos. 62509, 62515, 62519, 62520, 62523, 62533, 62538, 62562, 62620 and 62578 (at Melton Constable) and Nos. 62510, 62522, 62540, 62541, 62545, 62552, 62553, 62554, 62555, 62556, 62570, 62577, 62581, 62584, 62585, 62593, 62606, 62610, 62612, 62616, 62617, and 62619 at Norwich. Locally-based 'F6' 2–4–2Ts included Nos. 67224, 67225,

67228, 67229 and 67212, while other 2–4–2Ts seen on the branch included 'F4s' Nos. 67152, 67162, 67176 and 67178, together with 'F3' No. 67139.

Freight services were handled by a variety of ex-Great Eastern types, among them 'J15' 0–6–0s Nos. 65373, 65390, 65398, 65404, 65417, 65422, 65426, 65460, 65469 and 65479, 'J17' 0–6–0s Nos. 65507, 65509, 65512, 65513, 65516, 65553, 65568, 65569 and 65578, and 'J19' 0–6–0s Nos. 64644 and 64674.

Other types used on the Cromer line in the mid-1950s included large tank engines of BR, Great Central or LNER origin, and in this context it is interesting to note that, around 1953/4 'A5/1' 4–6–2Ts, 'V3' 2–6–2Ts or ex-LMS class '4MT' 2–6–4Ts were often seen heading Sheringham to Norwich or even Liverpool Street to Cromer trains. The Midland & Great Northern line, meanwhile, was worked by a mixture of ex-GER and other classes including Great Northern 'J1' and 'J6' 0–6–0s, and Great Central 'J11' 0–6–0s. Later, the line was worked by Ivatt class '4MT' 2–6–0s, which eventually replaced the older engines on most M&GN services.

Through workings brought additional locomotive types onto the East Norfolk route, and in this context 'B1', 'B12' and 'B17' 4–6–0s were particularly common on the "Norfolkman" and "Broadsman" expresses (which usually changed engines at Norwich). A summary of some of the principal classes used on the Cromer branch is given in Table 1 (*overleaf*).

The dieselisation of East Anglian branch lines began as early as the mid-1950s, one of the first routes to be dieselised being the North Walsham to Mundesley line, which was worked by conductor guards from the summer of 1956. This method of operation enabled BR to make various economies at Mundesley-on-Sea, where the signal box was reduced to ground frame status – the branch being worked thereafter on the "one-engine-in-steam" system with a train staff instead of the Tyers No. 6 tablet that had hitherto been provided.

The pace of dieselisation quickened in 1957–58, by which time further diesel multiple units had been drafted into the Norwich area for service on the Cromer branch and other local lines. At the same time, large main line diesels such as the D55XX Type 2 A1A–A1As (later class '31s') were appearing in increasing numbers, although these new locomotives did not replace steam completely, and the Cromer branch was worked by a mixture of steam and diesel power for several years.

From September 1958, the progressive introduction of 2,000 hp 1Co-Co1s on the Norwich main line enabled the Eastern Region to recast its timetables between London and Norwich with a regular interval service of fast trains, and by the beginning of 1959 the principal workings, including the "Norfolkman" and "Broadsman" services, were accelerated to provide a two-hour journey time between London and Norwich. The 1958–59 accelerations resulted, however, in a curtailment of through running onto the Cromer branch, and with most passenger services between Norwich, Cromer and Sheringham now handled by diesel multiple units, the "Broadsman" became the only remaining all year round through service between London and Sheringham.

TABLE 1
SUMMARY OF PRINCIPAL LOCOMOTIVE TYPES SEEN ON THE CROMER BRANCH c.1900–1966

Class	*Wheelbase*	*Notes*
'No. 1 Class'	2–4–0	Used on local services until about 1912.
Worsdell 'G14' class	2–4–0	Appeared at turn-of-the-century.
'T26' or 'E4' class	2–4–0	Succeeded the 'No. 1 class' and remained in regular use until recent years. Norwich had an allocation of 7 'E4s' in the early 1950s.
Holden '1000' class	2–2–2	Used on "Cromer Express".
Holden 'P43' class	4–2–0	Used on "Cromer Express" from 1898 until replaced by more powerful 'Claud Hamilton' 4–4–0s at the turn-of-the-century.
'Claud Hamilton' (LNER classes 'D15', 'D16/2', & 'D16/3')	4–4–0	Originally seen on the "Cromer Express" and other express workings, but were later cascaded onto more lowly duties, in which capacity they remained in everyday use until the BR era.
Worsdell 'Y14' class (LNER class 'J15')	0–6–0	Widely used on freight duties for many years.
Holden 'T19' class	2–4–0	Used on main line workings in Edwardian era.
'D13' class	4–4–0	Rebuilt 'T19s' used for many years on passenger workings.
Worsdell 'F4' class	2–4–2T	Used on passenger workings for many years.
Holden 'F3' class	2–4–2T	Used on passenger workings for many years.
Holden 'J17' class	0–6–0	Widely used on goods services.
'J19' class	0–6–0	Used on goods workings.
Holden 'S69' class	4–6–0	Initially used on the "Norfolk Coast Express" and other important passenger services, but later used on humbler workings.
Thompson 'B1' class	4–6–0	Worked through portions of the "Broadsman" and other expresses after their introduction in the 1940s.
Gresley 'Sandringham'	4–6–0	Used on main line workings.
Hill 'N7' class	0–6–2T	Worked on Mundesley branch.
'Britannia' Pacific	4–6–2	Sometimes seen north of Norwich, although it was usual for locomotives changes to take place at Norwich.
Holden 'F6' class	2–4–2T	Used on Mundesley branch.
Robinson 'A5' class	4–6–2T	Seen on Norwich–Cromer–Sheringham services in the British Railways era.
Gresley 'V3' class	2–6–2T	Appeared after World War II.
Fairburn '4MT' class	2–6–4T	Appeared in British Railways period.

The "Broadsman" express remained steam-worked north of Norwich, and on a sample day's running in the summer of 1959 an observer recorded that 1Co-Co1 No. D203 was replaced at Norwich by 'B1' 4–6–0 No. 61317 for the run to Cromer; on arrival at Cromer Beach the 'B1' was itself replaced by 'B17' 4–6–0 No. 61636 *Harlaxton Manor* for the final 3¾ mile leg of the journey to Sheringham.

The "Broadsman" was usually a nine-coach formation, and (presumably to expedite the two intermediate reversals at Norwich and Cromer) it was the practice to marshal a brake vehicle in the centre rather than at the ends of the set rakes. Leaving Cromer, the formation would typically be a second class vehicle, followed by a composite, a brake second, an open second, a dining car, a first class coach, another brake second, a further composite and finally an ordinary corridor second. The entire train was resplendent in the then-standard BR maroon livery, and like other Eastern Region named workings the "Broadsman" was formed of BR-built Mk. 1 stock.

Closure of the M&GN

The 1950s were, in many ways, a time of innovation and improvement, but ironically, the enhanced train services provided in that decade came at a time when road transport and government policies were poised to do irreparable harm to the railway industry. As mentioned above, BR initiated a policy of rationalisation in the early 1950s, but the minor closures of 1952–54 were designed to eliminate wasteful duplication and there was, at that time, no thought of introducing a widespread closure programme. Most people assumed that the recently-nationalised railways would be maintained in perpetuity, but this assumption was an illusion, and towards the end of the 1950s BR embarked on a ruthless pruning operation – the main victim being the Midland & Great Northern Joint Railway.

The M&GN enjoyed a brief Indian summer after World War II, but the writing had perhaps been on the wall ever since the LNER takeover in 1936; serving a rural area, far from main centres of population, the line had never been a money-spinner. Moreover, its seasonal holiday traffic from the Midlands to the Norfolk resorts could easily be diverted onto other routes. The LNER had started rationalising the M&GN before the war when it closed Melton Constable locomotive works and BR continued the process by pruning the coastal line back to Mundesley in 1953. With more and more people turning to alternative means of transport, and a government which made no secret of its hostility towards the nationalised railways, further contraction was inevitable. The blow came on Saturday, 28th February, 1959 when the M&GN was virtually wiped out, leaving a remnant between Melton Constable and Cromer Beach.

The Beeching Years

Government bias against rail transport reached its peak in March 1963, when the publication of Dr Richard Beeching's controversial report entitled *The Reshaping of British Railways* recommended the withdrawal of passenger services from 5,000 miles of line, together with the closure of no less than 2,363 stations. Local travellers consoled themselves with the thought that the Norwich to Cromer and Sheringham line did not appear in the initial list of doomed railways, although the Sheringham to Melton Constable section *was* listed as a closure victim. Elsewhere in East Anglia, the North Walsham to Mundesley-on-Sea line was threatened with closure, as were the branches to Aldeburgh, Maldon and Braintree.

Against this background of retraction and closure the Cromer branch seemed to have an assured future as one of Norfolk's few remaining coastal railheads, but closer analysis of the Beeching proposals revealed several worrying indications that did not bode well for the future. It was recommended, for instance, that extra trains should not be provided during peak holiday seasons, and furthermore, the spare rolling stock that had traditionally been held in reserve to cover holiday peaks would be withdrawn. Moreover, the report warned that the lines listed for immediate closure were only the "most hopelessly uneconomic ones", and the remaining branch lines would be "dealt with" [*sic*] after the first closures had been carried out.

The Beeching proposals were rushed into effect, and in April 1964 the Sheringham to Melton Constable section of the former M&GN was closed to passenger traffic. Goods services lingered on until the following December, but thereafter Sheringham became the terminus of the line from Norwich and Cromer. Meanwhile, the truncated Mundesley-on-Sea branch lost its passenger services on 3rd October, 1964, and remaining freight services were withdrawn at the end of the year.

The Post-Beeching Era

These retractions left the East Norfolk line in splendid isolation as the only passenger line for miles around; the only part of the M&GN still served by BR passenger trains was a 3¾ mile stub from Sheringham to Cromer which, with a small portion of the former Norfolk & Suffolk Joint between Runton East and Roughton Road Junctions, carried trains that continued over the former GE route to Norwich.

Although the Cromer branch was not axed in the Beeching era, it was not allowed to survive without further rationalisation of facilities. This was, at least in part, a direct result of surveys carried out within the Eastern Region in the mid-1960s which revealed that 90 per cent of all ER passenger traffic was generated by only 100 major stations. These findings were, on the face of it, hardly surprising in that stations such as Cromer and Sheringham did not in themselves contribute much in overall takings. On the other hand, they clearly attracted customers who travelled from major stations elsewhere on the system; a Londoner wishing to travel by rail to Cromer, for example, paid his fare at Liverpool Street, not at his destination. Indirectly, revenue was therefore generated by the provision of a rail link to the coast, and it was reasonable to assume that if that link did not exist then the journey might not have been made.

Disregarding this very real possibility, the Eastern Region proceeded to examine its East Anglian branch lines in greater detail, and after an exhaustive study of fares, ticketing, documentation and accounting, ER managers concluded that tickets sold at local stations were generally for short-distance journeys of less than a few miles. This appeared to indicate that traffic on surviving branch lines was self-contained, and faced with rising staff costs, the Eastern Region decided to work many of its East Anglian branches as "basic railways" with self-contained passenger services serving unstaffed halts.

In 1966 the neighbouring Hunstanton branch had the dubious distinction of becoming the first East Anglian "basic railway", with conductor-guards issuing only local tickets, and in 1967 a similar scheme was put into effect on the Norwich to Sheringham line. A corollary of these schemes was the abolition of most forms of cheap tickets and through booking facilities, while in physical terms the "basic railway" concept involved the elimination of several goods yards and a partial singling of the line. These changes were accompanied by the provision of a number of automatic level crossings between Norwich and North Walsham, and local residents were led to believe that this modest investment in new infrastructure underlined BR's long-term commitment to the East Norfolk route.

Meanwhile, the election of a new, less anti-railway government in October 1964 had brought an end to the Beeching closures, and the railway trade unions were confident that no Labour government would ever implement the kind of large-scale closure programme envisaged by the Marples-Beeching regime. Unfortunately, Mr Wilson's Labour administration was not as sympathetic as some commentators had predicted, and Transport Minister Barbara Castle's proposals (enabling socially-necessary routes to be subsidised by local authorities) did little to help rural lines such as the Cromer branch. Plans published in 1967 purported to show a "basic system" of about 11,000 route miles,[50] but on closer scrutiny, this revised railway network excluded many lines that had escaped the 1963 closure programme, and in Norfolk the basic system did *not* include the Lynn–Hunstanton, Lynn–Norwich or Norwich–Sheringham lines.

Significantly, most of Mrs Castle's "socially-necessary" railway services were concentrated in large urban conurbations which (perhaps by chance) happened to be areas where Labour voters were concentrated. The future for loss-making services in rural (and predominantly Tory) areas remained bleak, and at the beginning of 1968 BR published withdrawal notices for several supposedly-uneconomic branch line services in East Anglia – among them the Hunstanton and Cromer lines.[51] In this uncertain climate the once-busy Hunstanton branch was closed to all traffic on Saturday, 3rd May, 1969, and it seemed only a matter of time before the Norwich to Cromer line followed its neighbour into oblivion.

Happily, the pace of closure had slowed perceptibly after 1970, and in any case, the political situation was such that politicians were reluctant to antagonise voters by closing railways when governments were themselves struggling for survival. The minority Labour government, for example, faced an election in 1970, while two years later Mr Heath went to the country against a background of strikes and power cuts.

There was, moreover, a feeling that the Beeching axe had been swung too widely, and when the 1973–74 oil crisis finally tipped the balance towards energy-efficient forms of transport, the future of the Cromer branch seemed relatively secure. Having narrowly escaped closure in 1968–69, the East Norfolk line was awarded a 3-year grant of £133,000 under section 39 of the 1968 Transport Act, and as a recipient of grant aid the line has remained part of the BR network.

The train service provided in recent years has been fairly constant, with a basic frequency of about 12–13 trains each way on weekdays, and a reduced Sunday service of around 4 workings each way. All passenger workings are composed of diesel multiple unit stock – ostensibly because of weight restrictions over bridges between Norwich and Cromer.

In May 1972 there were 12 up and 12 down trains between Norwich and Cromer, together with a solitary short-distance working between Norwich and North Walsham; 9 trains continued through to Sheringham after reversing at Cromer Beach, while 3 workings terminated at Cromer.

Methods of operation were surprisingly complex. The daily timetable began with an early morning departure from Norwich at 5.21 am, and this first down service arrived at Sheringham at 6.17 am. The flexibility inherent in multiple unit operation allowed the train to "turn round" in just five minutes, and at 6.22 am the dmu returned to Cromer. Meanwhile, a second train from Norwich had arrived in Cromer at 6.32 am, and having passed the 6.22 from Sheringham, the two trains resumed their respective journeys. A third down train was, by this time, *en route* to Sheringham, and at 6.52 am this train passed the 6.22 am ex-Sheringham in the crossing loop at North Walsham. The train from Sheringham arrived in Norwich at 7.22 am, and there were, thereafter, further departures from Norwich to Cromer or Sheringham at 7.38, 9.18, 11.35 am, 1.52, 3.36, 5.20, 5.57, 7.47 and 9.14 pm. In the reverse direction, corresponding up workings left Cromer at 7.13, 7.47, 8.32, 10.37 am, 12.50, 3.42, 4.28, 6.51, 7.56, 9.24 and 10.07 pm.

It will be seen that, despite the rationalisation of facilities in 1966–67, the Cromer branch did not become a complete "basic railway", and with freight traffic still being handled at Wroxham, North Walsham and Cromer Beach, the branch retained much of its signalling and trackwork. There was still a section of double track between Whitlingham Junction and Wroxham, while Wroxham and North Walsham stations retained their yard sidings and other connections. At Cromer, the former GER terminus at Cromer High remained in use as a goods yard until 1960, while Cromer Beach retained its goods facilities for a few more years, finally succumbing to rationalisation after coal traffic had been concentrated in a new purpose-built yard on the site of Norwich Victoria station.

Summer Saturday through trains were not immediately withdrawn, and in 1972 the branch was still served by a train which left Liverpool Street at 10.04 am and arrived in Sheringham at 2.07 pm. In the reverse direction, a balancing up working left Sheringham at 2.42 pm, and having called at Cromer at 2.51, the train – usually a six-car formation – arrived back in London by 6.22 pm. For holidaymakers, this residual through working no doubt served a useful purpose in that harassed travellers did not have to change trains at Norwich, but the dmu's slow speed (little short of 4 hours in the down direction) was pitiful. Needless to say, buffet facilities were not provided, and the 10.04 from London could not, in any way, stand comparison with the glamorous through trains of years gone by. On a footnote, it may be worth adding that this summer-only dmu train made an out-and-back journey of 291 miles without servicing.

For travellers in a hurry, the best journey times between London and Cromer were available, not on the 10.04 am (SO), but by means of the 9.30 am express from Liverpool Street; this train – in effect the old "Norfolkman" – reached Norwich at 11.30 am, and provided a useful connection with the 11.35 Norwich to Sheringham dmu, which arrived in Cromer at 12.23 pm (i.e. 2 hours 53 minutes from London).

Recent Developments

The May 1982 timetable was similar to its 1972 predecessor, with 13 trains each way between Norwich and Cromer on weekdays and 4 in each direction on Sundays. The unsatisfactory summer Saturday through train no longer ran, but prospective through travellers were offered a range of useful connecting services between London and Norwich. A journey time of less than three hours was available on Fridays when the last down train from Norwich provided a connection with the 7.30 pm express from Liverpool Street, and by changing at Norwich it was possible to be in Cromer by 10.23 pm or Sheringham by 10.35 pm.

In contrast to most other rural branch lines, The Cromer route has, in recent years, been of interest to modern traction enthusiasts in that large main line diesel locomotives still regularly appear. In September 1961 a new connection was provided at Themelthorpe, and this enabled surviving M&GN goods traffic to be diverted onto the ex-GER County School branch and thence via Wroxham, to Norwich. In the next few years the Themelthorpe–Wroxham line carried a relatively heavy traffic in pre-cast concrete components from a factory in Lenwade (on the former M&GN Norwich branch). Indeed, some of these workings were so heavy that double-heading was resorted to, and it was not uncommon for two class '31' A1A–A1As to be seen working in tandem at the head of long trains of bogie bolsters. Sadly, this lucrative bulk traffic ceased running in 1982, but the Cromer branch still carries bulk freight traffic in the form of gas-condensate from North Walsham. Agricultural products are also carried to and from Wroxham goods yard, and for these reasons it is possible to see class '31s' or class '37s' in regular use on the former East Norfolk line. Another source of traffic – albeit of a more sporadic nature – is generated by Crane Fruehauf Trailers of North Walsham, who manufacture containers used by Canadian Pacific and other shipping lines.

Passenger services are handled by Cravens, Metro-Cammell, or Birmingham RC&W units, although it would probably be true to say that Metro-Cammell 'class 101' sets have become the most characteristic types on the Cromer branch. More recently, in November 1985, the first "Sprinter" unit reached the East Norfolk route when set No. 150 001 worked through to Sheringham during a programme of trips around north Norfolk local lines.

Having described the history of the East Norfolk line from its inception until the present day, it would now be appropriate to examine the route of the branch in greater detail. The following chapter will therefore take readers on an imaginary journey from Norwich Thorpe to Cromer and thence along the former M&GN line to Sheringham. (Topographical details will be correct for the early 1980s, but as stated in the introduction, some details may be out of date by the time that this work appears in print).

Sources for Chapter 5

48 *The Railway Magazine*, March 1954 p.212.
49 E. Tuddenham, The Norfolk & Suffolk Joint, *Railway World* July 1966 p.292.
50 *The Railway Magazine*, May 1967 pp.250–54.
51 *Ibid*. January 1968 p.54.

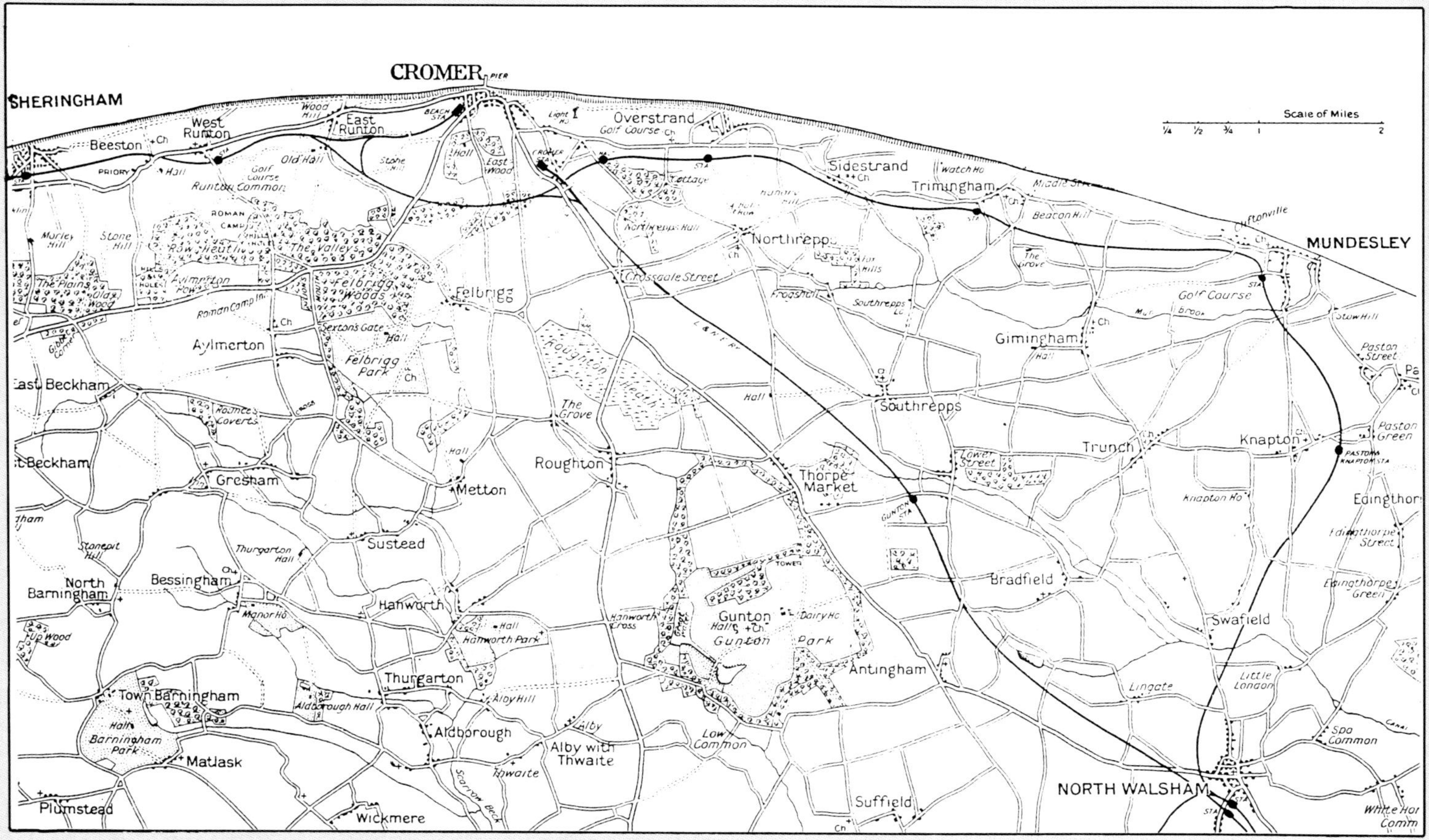

Details of the railway network serving Cromer. Courtesy *Ward Lock & Co., Red Guide*

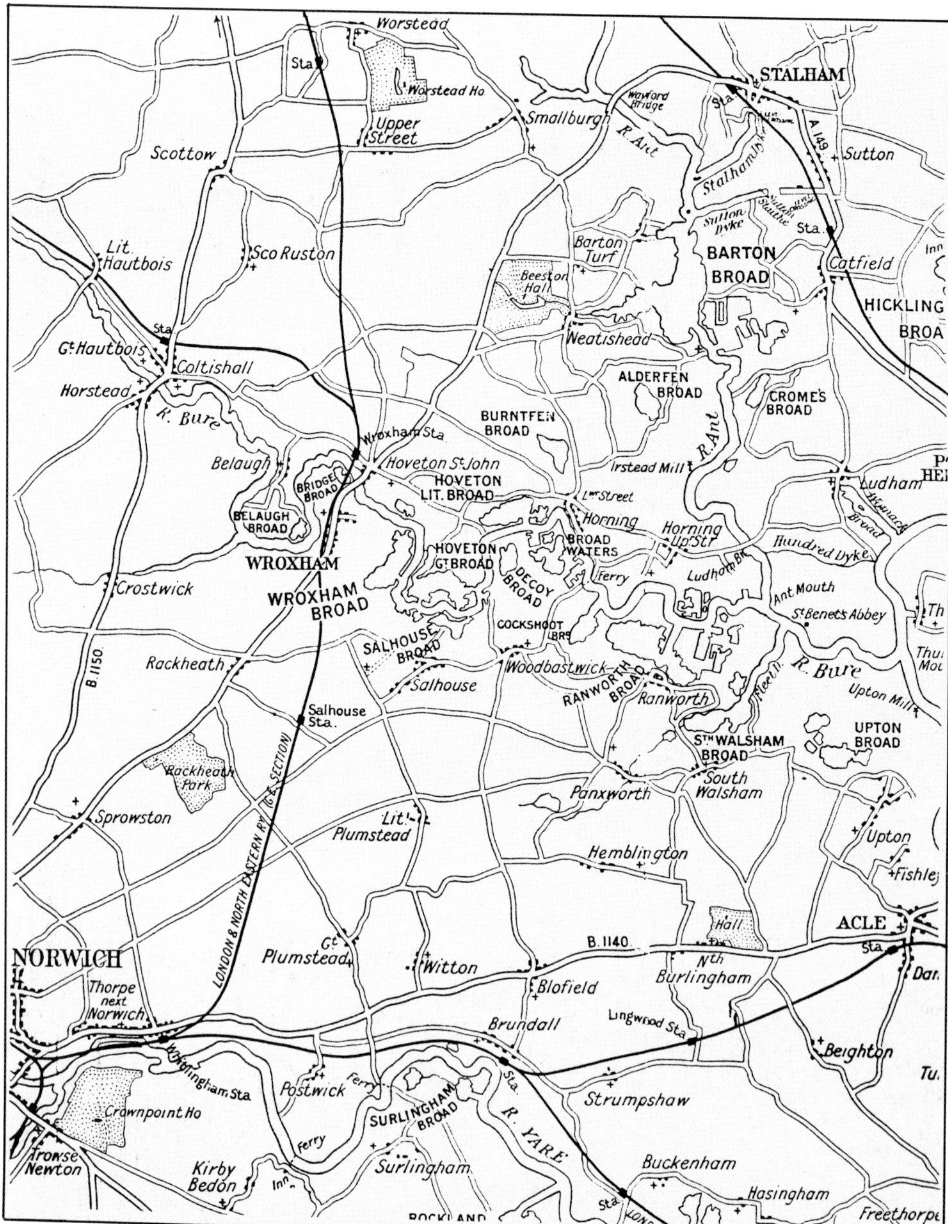

Map of the line from North Walsham to Norwich

Courtesy Ward Lock & Co., Red Guide

The "Central European" facade of Norwich Thorpe station. Designed by W.N. Ashbee, the building was damaged in World War Two, but nevertheless retains its original appearance. *D. Thompson*

Norwich Station seen here in the Edwardian era, showing typical GER 6-wheeled coaching stock. *Lens of Sutton*

Two views of Norwich Thorpe station, captured on film in March 1948.
Mowat Collection

No. 61270 awaiting departure on the 31st August, 1951 from Norwich Thorpe Station.
H.C. Casserley

Chapter Six

The Route Described

Norwich Thorpe, the southern terminus of most Cromer branch services, is a comparatively modern station, and the present terminal building with its towering dome and ornate *porte cochère* was erected as recently as the 1880s. In architectural terms, the building is of distinctly central European appearance, and one feels that its vaguely Hapsburgian features should have been built, not in Norfolk, but at some important station in Bohemia or Slovakia! On closer examination, the essential symmetry of the main façade has been compromised by the removal of part of the roof at one end of the building – a result of bomb damage in World War II.

In operational terms, Norwich Thorpe is more modest than its outwards appearance would suggest, and behind the lavish architectural façade, the station incorporates just two main island platforms, giving four platform faces for trains to London, Yarmouth, Cromer and the Midlands. Two additional platforms have seen little use since the withdrawal of services to Kings Lynn and Wells-next-the-Sea in the 1960s, but the terminus is still surprisingly busy, and in the 1980s Norwich handled around 80 trains a day. The station was extensively refurbished in 1974–75 when, as part of a programme of improvements, the Victorian brickwork was sand-blasted and new passenger accommodation was provided.

More recently, Norwich underwent further modernisation in connection with the extension of 25,000 volt ac overhead electrification from Ipswich. The scheme was officially launched on 5th May, 1987, when a seven-coach inaugural special ran from Liverpool Street to Norwich, covering the intervening 115 miles in only 83 minutes 22 seconds – a record for the GER main line.

As a concomitant of electrification, BR had earlier opened a new £10 million locomotive and rolling stock depot at Crown Point, to the east of the passenger station; the depot was formally opened by Sir Peter Parker, then chairman of BR, on 27th October, 1982. The Crown Point complex covers twelve acres, and provides facilities for cleaning and general maintenance of locomotives, carriages and dmu stock. Most of these operations take place under one roof, and to allow adequate room for entire trains, the main building is 270 yds long.

Leaving Norwich Thorpe, Cromer trains initially head south-eastwards to Thorpe Junction, at which point the line divides, with one route diverging south towards Ipswich, while the other arm continues due east towards Great Yarmouth. With Crown Point maintenance depot visible to the right, Cromer trains follow the Yarmouth line, and are soon running beside the River Yare; to the left, the busy A47 road can be seen beside the railway, and road, river and railway continue on a more or less parallel course for a distance of about two miles.

At Wensum Junction – a short distance beyond Thorpe Junction – the direct, north-to-south curve converges from the right. This short line was opened on 1st October, 1879, and its presence was an immense advantage for the Cromer line, in that main line services were able to run direct from Cromer to London without reversing in Norwich Thorpe.

Bridge No. 358 between Whitlingham and Norwich photographed in February 1926.
Oakwood Collection

Whitlingham Junction looking east from the cab of 79050/266. The East Norfolk line can be seen diverging to the left.
H.B. Priestley

Whitlingham

Although most Cromer branch trains ran to or from Norwich, there was formerly a station near the divergence of the Cromer and Yarmouth lines at Whitlingham Junction. Situated immediately to the west of East Norfolk Junction, Whitlingham was a two platform stopping place, with limited goods facilities. Whitlingham was nevertheless of some interest in that it was near the site of one of Britain's worst head-on collisions, which occurred on the night of 10th September, 1874 when a down Norwich express collided with an up mail.

The drama began at 9.30 pm when an evening express from London to Norwich was allowed to proceed on to the Norwich to Yarmough line on the final leg of its journey to Great Yarmouth. The Yarmouth line was, at that time, a single track route, and although a second line of rails was already *in situ* pending completion of the Cromer Branch, the new line had not yet been "passed" for opening. In the meantime, up and down trains were able to cross at Brundall, and, with the aid of Cooke & Wheatstone telegraph instruments, this method of operation had worked in perfect safety for 26 years.

Sadly, the system broke down on the fateful night of Thursday, 10th September, 1874, when, due to conflicting instructions, a Norwich station inspector ordered a junior telegraph clerk to let a westbound train enter the single line section while that section was occupied by the down express. Realising the magnitude of their error, the Norwich officials telegraphed Brundall in a futile attempt to cancel the previous instruction, but when Brundall's station master replied with the ominous message "Mail Gone", there was no hope of averting a major catastrophe.

Events now moved with inevitable swiftness as the express, headed by Gooch "Butterfly" 2–4–0 No. 218, thundered eastwards into the night, while the Mail raced westwards behind Sinclair single No. 54. Too late, the driver of No. 218 tried to throw his engine into reverse while the crew of the mail train frantically screwed down their tender brake. The impact took place near Thorpe village, and with a "noise like thunder" No. 218 ploughed into the speeding mail train, both trains being violently thrown from the line. Fire broke out immediately, and *The Yarmouth Independent* described the disaster as follows:

> On the train from Yarmouth and Lowestoft reaching Mr Stephen Field's boathouse, situate almost opposite the well-known Thorpe Gardens, the train from Norwich dashed into it with a fearful velocity, the terrible force of the collision causing in a moment of time a scene of wreck and ruin such has seldom been witnessed at the most horrible of railway accidents that have taken place of late years in this country.

Victorian journalists and technical experts were shocked at the effects of the collision, which had resulted in the more or less total destruction of two complete trains. On 26th September, 1874 *The Railway Times* printed a clinical assessment of the damage:

> The funnels and smoke-boxes of both engines were carried away. The cylinders of

Salhouse station, looking south towards Norwich; this recent view does not show the now-demolished signal box which used to stand at the southern end of the up platform. *Lens of Sutton*

Salhouse station, looking north towards Cromer, and showing the Great Eastern waiting room on the up side (*right*). To the left, the ENR wooden building shows a contrasting style of wooden construction. *Lens of Sutton*

> both engines were slightly forced out of position; the wheels of the express engine were also forced a little out of shape. The tanks were knocked away from the under frames of both engines. As regards the damage to the stock, there were thirteen vehicles destroyed and four damaged. The vehicles destroyed in the train from Norwich were third class, composite, and second class carriages, and a horse box. In the Yarmouth train the carriages destroyed were a brake van, third class, and composite carriages and a mail van. There were two brake vans and two guards in each train beside the tender brakes.[52]

In all, 25 people were killed in the disaster, including the crews of both locomotives. A further 73 people were injured, many seriously, in this, the worst accident in Great Eastern history.

Salhouse

Leaving the site of this appalling Victorian tragedy, present day trains turn leftwards onto the Cromer branch at East Norfolk Junction, and with the outer suburbs of Norwich still visible to the left, the double track branch is carried across the busy A47 road on a substantial overbridge.

Climbing steadily at 1 in 80, the route runs through cuttings before crossing a minor road on another overbridge. Beyond, the line passes through further cuttings, but these soon give way to a tract of open country as the route reaches a succession of closely-spaced level crossings – the first of which carries trains across the relatively busy B1140, while the others cross country roads of somewhat less importance.

Heading through pleasant Norfolk countryside, trains continue along the branch towards Salhouse, the first intermediate station. Serving a small Broadland settlement, Salhouse is 5 miles 74 chains from Norwich Thorpe; the station has up and down platforms, its main station building, of wooden construction, being on the down side. The goods yard (now lifted) was on the down side of the line; no goods shed, cattle dock, or yard crane was provided, but the single goods siding could be entered, by crossovers, from either the up or the down main lines.

When first opened in 1874, Salhouse had consisted of little more than a single passenger platform, together with a short goods siding; an up platform was added in 1891, and the station reached its final form when the line was doubled in 1896. In architectural terms, Salhouse is an amalgam of East Norfolk and late-Victorian GER structures – the hip-roofed, timber building on the down platform being of ENR vintage while its brick-built counterpart on the up side is of Great Eastern origin.

As mentioned in *Chapter One*, Lucas Brothers (who, as contractors were responsible for the building of the East Norfolk line) were specialists in the use of pre-fabrication. Their characteristic, weather-boarded buildings were manufactured in large numbers for a variety of purposes including office accommodation, navvies' huts and even military barracks in the Crimea. These buildings were the cheapest available in 1874, and there was a high degree of standardisation in terms of window frames, internal structure and general dimensions; there seems little doubt that Salhouse's main station building originated in Lucas Brothers' workshops – although the projecting platform canopy, with its huge metal spandrels, is clearly a Great Eastern addition.

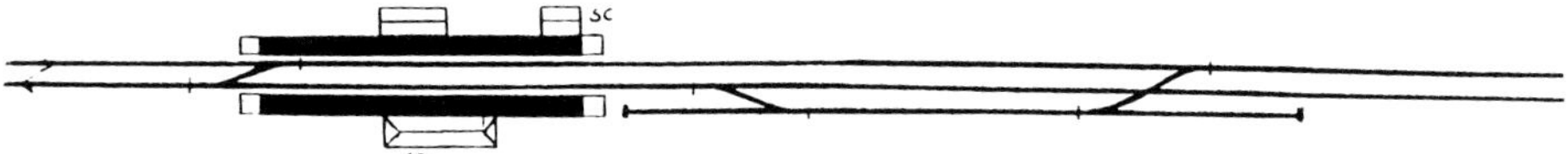

SALHOUSE

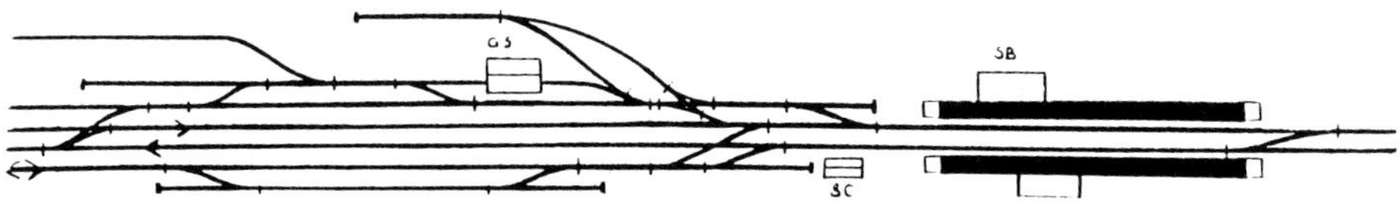

WROXHAM

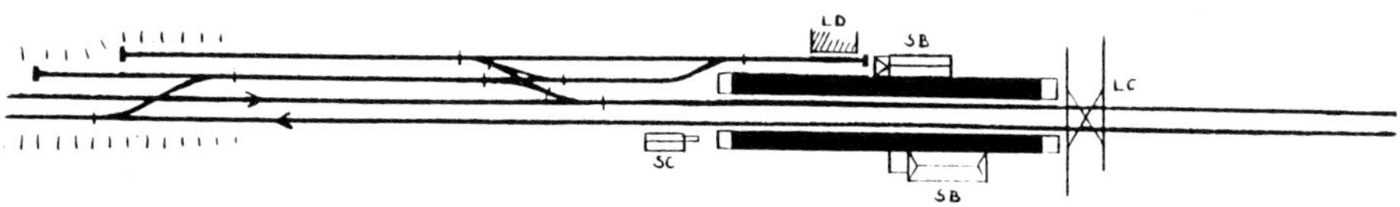

WORSTEAD

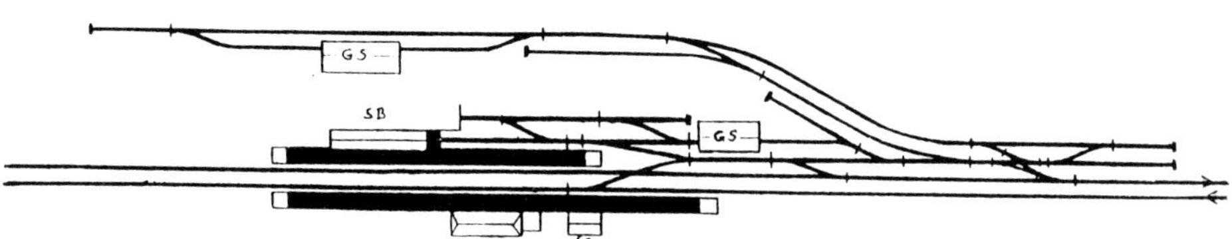

NORTH WALSHAM

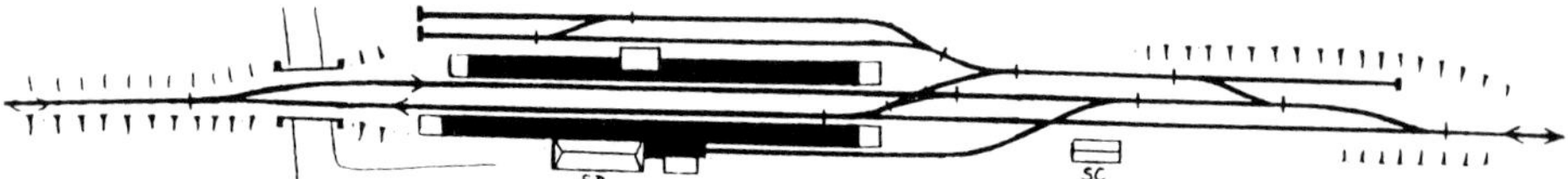

GUNTON

Diagrammatic station layouts, *c*.1920.

The northern end of the platforms at Wroxham station, showing the goods yard in the right distance. *Lens of Sutton*

Wroxham station, looking south towards Norwich, with the replacement station building on the left. *Lens of Sutton*

The much smaller, brick-built waiting room on the up platform, is a typical Great Eastern building, owing much to the late-Victorian "vernacular revival"; it was probably designed by W.N. Ashbee, the GER architect (or by someone in his department). The signal box, on the up side, was also of typical Great Eastern appearance – although, in this case, the lower storey was of brick construction instead of the more usual timber; the box had 20 levers, and was abolished in 1967.

Like other country stations Salhouse was once a significant employment centre in a rural area; the statiion master here in 1888 was George William Smith, but by the middle-1890s Mr Smith had been replaced by Charles Notley – who was himself replaced by William Smith in the Edwardian period.

Wroxham

From Salhouse, the route continues northwards, crossing a minor road on an overbridge and then a country lane on the level. Approaching Wroxham, trains enter some comparatively deep cuttings that are spanned, at one point, by the A1151 road which crosses the railway before running parallel on the eastern side of the line. A short distance further on, trains cross the River Bure on a long, brick and girder viaduct.

Wroxham, the next stopping place, is an important intermediate station, some 8 miles 60 chains from Norwich. Perhaps surprisingly, this station retained its junction status until the 1980s, the former East Norfolk branch to County School having survived for many years as a freight-only route as far as Lenwade until 1982; the abandoned branch was finally lifted in 1984.

Always an important station, Wroxham had been a two-platform stopping place even in East Norfolk days. There was no separate bay for County School branch trains, but the track layout at this rural junction was large enough to justify the provision of two signal boxes. The main box, dating from around 1900, replaced an earlier signal cabin that had formerly been sited on the up platform; known as the "station box", this new cabin housed a 50-lever frame. A smaller signal box, known as the "yard box", contained 23 levers, but this subsidiary cabin was later abolished, and thereafter the station box controlled Wroxham's entire layout.[53] The box remained in commission after the 1967 track-rationalisation – although by that time half of its levers were white-painted "spares".

Like other East Norfolk stations, Wroxham was originally provided with wooden "contractors' style" buildings, but these were later supplemented by the addition of a brick-built GER building on the down side. Later still, the wooden ENR building was taken down and in its place the LNER erected a somewhat ugly, flat-topped structure with a projecting platform canopy. The station is situated in an elevated position on a low embankment, and intending travellers have to ascend to platform level via flights of steps.

Victorian railway men often moved from station to station in pursuit of higher pay or status, and this was particularly true of clerical grades who – after a period of "apprenticeship" as junior clerks – were expected to seek more rewarding posts elsewhere. Having reached the coveted position of

Worstead station, looking south towards the Great Eastern style level crossing with its single-span timber gates. *Lens of Sutton*

Worstead's main station building was a wooden ENR structure, to which a GER canopy was later attached; the vertical timber laths to which the spandrels were bolted can be glimpsed in this *c*.1962 view. *D. Thompson*

station master, some employees settled down, and it was not uncommon for individuals to remain for twenty or more years at one station. This was certainly the case at Wroxham, where as we have seen, Francis Underhill remained in charge from the 1870s until World War I – a period of almost forty years! A later station master, around 1922, was Robert Lawrence who came to Wroxham from Whitlingham Junction.

The trackwork at Wroxham is, even today, quite extensive, and several sidings remain *in situ* to deal with agricultural traffic. Wroxham is now the northernmost limit of double track operation, the sections beyond having been reduced to single track in 1967. More recently, Wroxham was renamed Hoveton & Wroxham – a logical move because the station serves both places (and is, in any case, nearer to Hoveton than Wroxham).

Wroxham itself is a popular Broadland tourist centre – it is, if anything, rather *too* popular, and at the height of the summer season, the discerning traveller will be glad when his train gains the single line section north of the station, and heads towards the quieter, more rural areas beyond.

The County School line ran parallel to the "main line" for about a quarter of a mile (giving the impression that the line was still double tracked), but this abandoned line soon diverges to the west, and the Cromer route is left to penetrate the wilds alone. Maintaining its northerly heading, the branch traverses a remote, rural area, punctuated by a further succession of level crossings carrying minor roads across the railway. Down trains soon reach another embankment which is pierced by an underbridge; beyond, the route is carried across a minor road on the level before the embankments resume once more on the approaches to Worstead.

Worstead

Worstead, 13 miles 9 chains from Norwich, is the next stop. Once a centre of the Norfolk woollen industry, it is now a quiet rural place with a fine Medieval church (begun in 1369) to remind us of its erstwhile importance.

Like other stations on the branch, Worstead is now an unstaffed halt and only its former up platform remains in use. Until rationalisation the goods yard, also on the up side, had incorporated a somewhat complex arrangement of loops and crossovers, by means of which the yard could be shunted by either up or down trains. Sadly, all of this Victorian infrastructure has now been obliterated, and in common with many other country stations, Worstead is merely a shadow of its former self.

Like Salhouse, Worstead station exhibited an interesting mixture of East Norfolk and Great Eastern architecture. The main booking office and waiting rooms were accommodated in a squat, hip-roofed, wooden building on the down side, and this somewhat austere structure was clearly a relic of the ENR; the solid, brick-built waiting room on the up platform was, in contrast a Great Eastern addition, as was the standard, timber-built GER signal cabin. Other typical Great Eastern features included the station's simple, wooden-posted oil lamps, and the huge level crossing gates at the south end of the platforms.

As usual on Great Eastern lines, the crossing had only one set of gates, and the resulting gates were of enormous size and weight, necessitating massive diagonal bracing which was arranged with the aid of huge, white-painted wooden gate posts (although primarily a structural feature, these prominent white posts also gave drivers a useful visual indication when approaching each crossing).

Worstead's station master in the late 1880s was Frederick William Avery, and like his counterpart at Wroxham, Mr Avery enjoyed a long association with the Cromer branch; he was still in office during World War I, but had been replaced, at the time of the 1923 grouping, by Charles Wilby. Other locally-employed railwaymen included signalman G. Allard, signalman E. Grimes, and porter-signalman Herbert Baldry who, on 3rd March, 1911, had the misfortune to be injured by a tow rope while trying to uncouple a string of moving coal wagons in Worstead goods yard (reporting on this accident, the BoT Inspector suggested that the use of tow ropes "might be considerably reduced").

North Walsham

Leaving Worstead, trains continue northwards through attractive, gently undulating countryside, running first on embankments and then in cuttings as they approach North Walsham. To the right, the busy A149 road now occupies part of the abandoned Midland & Great Northern Joint trackbed.

Situated some 15 miles 77 chains from Norwich Thorpe, North Walsham is still a comparatively busy freight and passenger station, and its goods sidings, which fan out into an extensive yard on the up side, usually contain plenty of tank wagons. These convey gas condensate which is piped from a terminal at Bacton via a pipeline buried beneath the former Mundesley-on-Sea branch.

A passing place on the single line section between Wroxham and Cromer, North Walsham has retained its long crossing loop; up and down platforms are provided, the main brick-built station buildings being on the up side. A standard GER gabled signal cabin remains in use of the down platform, and a large red brick goods shed survives intact in the nearby goods yard.

North Walsham itself is a growing country town of around 10,000 inhabitants but there is little to see, apart from the fine Perpendicular church and an unusual market cross, with a cupola and weather vane. The town's 17th century grammar school is famous through its association with Horatio Nelson, who was a pupil until he joined the Royal Navy at the age of twelve. Still on a martial theme, it is interesting to recall that during World War I, North Walsham was used as a base by the armoured train mentioned in Chapter Three.

Accelerating away from North Walsham, Cromer trains cross the abandoned M&GN line and then head north into a particularly remote stretch of north Norfolk countryside. Those travelling in the front saloons will note a distinct narrowing of the trackbed on this final section of line, which was always single track. This section of the route is heavily engineered, and cuttings alternate with embankments as the railway enters a belt of higher land that surrounds Cromer.

North Walsham station had substantial brick buildings on both up and down platforms, together with the standard GER signal cabin; a 'J15' 0–6–0 can be seen heading southwards in this *c.*1930s view. *Lens of Sutton*

A view south from the up platform at North Walsham, showing the standard GER signal cabin and goods shed. *Lens of Sutton*

Detail of the north end of the platforms at North Walsham station, showing the subway entrances and roof of the low-level station buildings. *Lens of Sutton*

North Walsham station looking southwards to Norwich on the 27th May, 1958. Note the curious bay windows on the signal box for better visibility. *H.B. Priestley*

The attractive main station building at Gunton; this hip-roofed structure was designed to accommodate Lord Suffield's guests, for which purpose it was more lavishly-equipped than other ENR stations. *Lens of Sutton*

Gunton station in November 1963, with GER lamp posts and other fittings still in place. *D. Thompson*

Gunton

Gunton, the penultimate station, is 19 miles 61 chains from Norwich. It was once a passing place on the 7 mile section of single line beyond North Walsham, but today, all sidings and connections are lifted. The main building, on the former down platform, is a hipped roof structure with a projecting canopy; internally, its decor was of ornate, Tudor appearance – in which respect the station was quite out of character with the small villages that it purported to serve.

Significantly, Gunton Park, the seat of Lord Suffield, was less than two miles away, and this does much to explain the palatial nature of the station accommodation! Indeed, Gunton had much in common with Wolferton, on the neighbouring Hunstanton branch (which was designed for the reception of royalty and other VIP guests). Although Lord Suffield's local station was not as heavily-used as Wolferton, it was clearly intended to be used by important travellers, who would perhaps have been insulted by the thought of mingling with common folk at an ordinary rural station.

In common with other East Anglian country stations, Gunton's track layout was, until rationalisation, surprisingly complex, with ample siding accommodation for grain and other agricultural traffic. In its heyday, the station had a long passing loop, with up and down platforms on either side, and an additional goods loop and two sidings to the east. A further dead-end siding served an end-loading dock behind the down platform, and the signal box, also on the down side, was a standard Great Eastern gabled structure, similar to others provided on the branch.

Today, the station ekes out a meagre living as an unstaffed halt, and the extensive station buildings have found a new lease of life as a private dwelling; all trains now use the former up platform, the down side having been taken out of use in 1966–67.

Cromer Beach

The northernmost section of the branch traverses what is, by East Anglian standards, decidedly hilly country, and heavy earthworks predominate all the way to Cromer. Soon, the small seaside town can be seen clustered round its grey Church tower, with the North Sea beyond – though as trains approach their destination dense foliage limits the view.

At Cromer Junction, the original line to Cromer High diverges northwards, but present day trains swing west to gain the GER and M&GN joint route at Roughton Road Junction, where the abandoned coastal line from Mundesley formerly converged from the east. The trackwork hereabouts was once surprisingly complex, and present-day travellers, gazing at the overgrown cuttings that now mark the site of Cromer Junction, may find it hard to believe that there was formerly a double track junction in this otherwise unremarkable place. From Cromer Junction, the double line continued to Roughton Road, where the converging lines were controlled from an ornate signal box with a curious pagoda-type roof (said to have been provided to appease an anti-railway landowner).

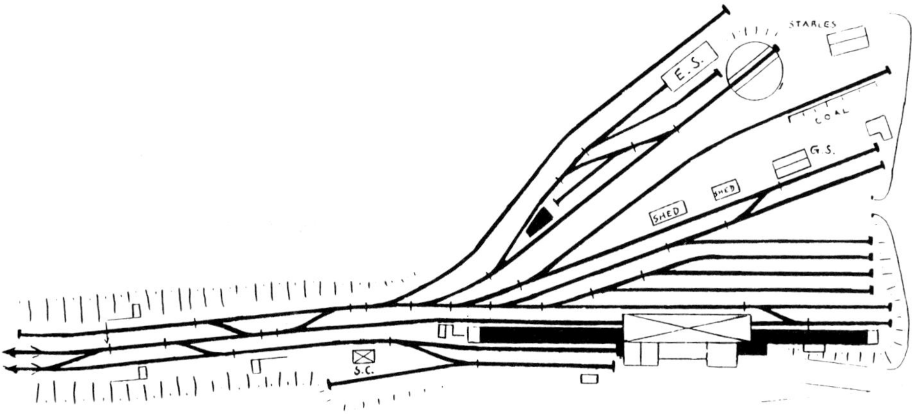

CROMER BEACH

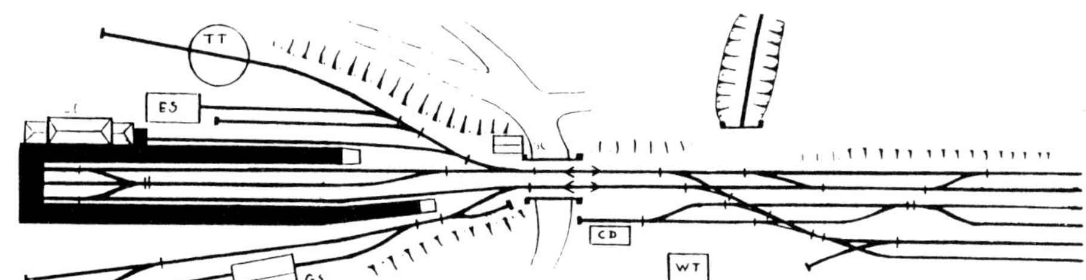

CROMER HIGH

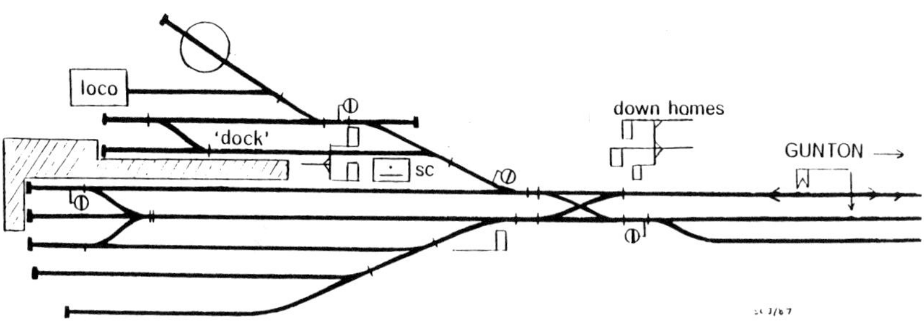

CROMER c1887

Top and *centre*; track layouts at Cromer Branch and Cromer High; *bottom* a diagrammatic signalling layout at Cromer in the 19th Century.

An early view of Cromer Beach. The flat-bottomed trackwork (used by the Eastern & Midlands Railway) can be glimpsed in this *c.*1890s photograph. *Oakwood Collection*

A Metro-Cammell multiple unit (now class 101) departs from Cromer Beach station in July 1968; the train is running on the main line, and will shortly diverge rightwards onto the Sheringham line; note the tablet catchers beyond the platform. *S.C. Jenkins*

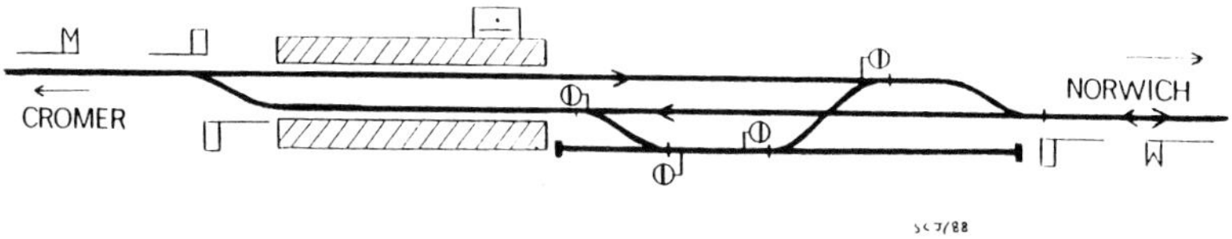

SALHOUSE
c 1891

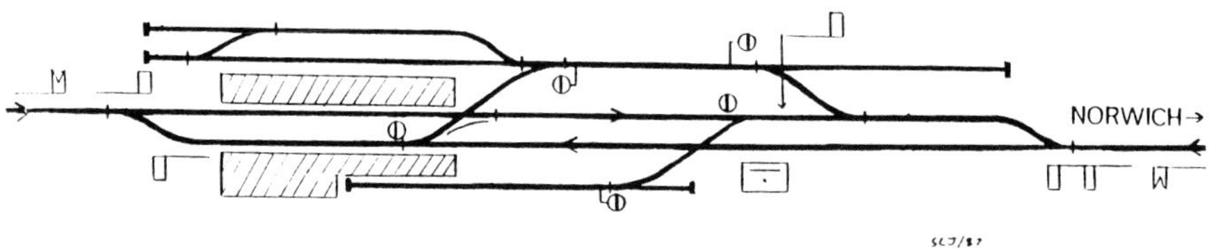

GUNTON

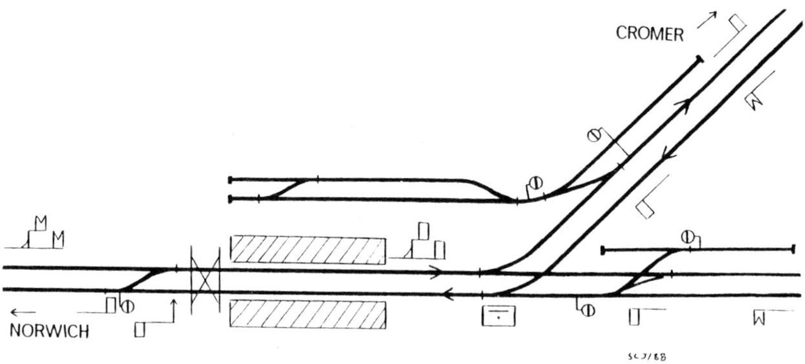

WHITLINGHAM JCT.

Signal box diagrams for Salhouse, Gunton and Whitlingham Jct.

A view of Cromer Beach station approach road, note the brick infilling (or "brick nogging") visible behind the Refreshment Room sign. The ironwork on this side of the building incorporates the initials "M & GN" whereas spandrels on the other side bear the letters "E & MR". *Real Photographs*

Detail of the "E & MR" spandrels at Cromer Beach. *H.N. James*

The northernmost end of Cromer Beach's main platform. This Edwardian view shows a wealth of detail, including flat-bottomed track *in situ* (*right*), ornate gas lamps, Midland-type fencing and an M & GN horse box. *Real Photographs*

An interesting panoramic view of Cromer Beach at the turn-of-the-Century; note that, although the station had ample storage sidings, its platform consisted of nothing more than a long main platform and short bay (*right*). *Real Photographs*

No. 8087 at Cromer Beach in August 1937. *J. Kite*

The 19.52 from Sheringham to Norwich rounds the curve into Cromer Beach in July 1968; the branch is at this point worked as 2 single lines, the Norwich line being on the right while the Sheringham line is to the left. *S.C. Jenkins*

In 1985, a new halt was opened at Roughton Road to serve growing residential developments on the southern outskirts of Cromer, and it may be that this new station will ultimately become Cromer's main station – serving car-borne commuters who (if adequate parking is available) will drive in from the surrounding area rather than walk to the existing station at Cromer Beach. In operational terms, the idea of an improved station at Roughton Road would make good sense insofar as it is on the direct line to Sheringham. On the other hand, BR may be reluctant to spend considerable sums of money on the reinstatement of a southern curve between Newstead Lane and Runton West Junction, and in these circumstances it seems likely that trains will continue to use Cromer Beach for the foreseeable future.

Encircling Cromer, the line reaches a former triangular junction with large, arched viaducts on two sides, before trains slow for the final crawl into Cromer Beach. Passing the site of Newstead Lane Junction, present-day dmus take the east curve – a glance to the left reveals the abandoned south curve which formerly rejoined the Cromer–Sheringham line at Runton West Junction. With the Sheringham line now running parallel to the left, the line snakes through massive cuttings before terminating in the long, main platform at Cromer Beach. Here, in a station first used by trains of the Eastern & Midlands Railway in 1887, the 26 mile 54 chain journey from Norwich to Cromer comes to an end.

In pre-Beeching days, Cromer Beach had boasted extensive carriage sidings, together with a modest goods yard and a single-road engine shed, but today, all superfluous trackwork has been removed, leaving little more than the main platform road and a short bay. The station buildings are unusual in that they are timber-framed in Victorian–Tudor style. A small overall roof covers the platform immediately in front of the buildings, and eagle-eyed travellers will note the initials "E&MR" in the spandrels. Walking from the platform to the carriageway, however, observant enthusiasts will see that the ironwork on this side of the station was erected later than 1893, as it bears the letters "M&GN".

In its early days the station's entire track layout was laid with flat-bottomed rail spiked directly to transverse wooden sleepers, and in this respect the M&GN terminus was unlike its Great Eastern rival, which had conventional bullhead trackwork. Amusingly, many Victorian railwaymen disliked flat-bottomed trackwork, which was castigated as "Yankee" or "contractors" rail – and perhaps for this reason, Great Eastern men often referred to the M&GN as "the tramway"!

The station had been relaid with bullhead rail by the end of the 19th century, but apart from this routine renewal of time-expired equipment the basic track layout remained unchanged until the summer of 1954. In that year Cromer Beach was extensively remodelled in connection with the closure of Cromer High and a corresponding increase of traffic at the former M&GN terminus. Work carried out at that time included doubling of the station approaches, lengthening of the platform, and extensive signalling alterations; new brackets were provided for the down home and up starters, and 14 new ground shunt signals were installed. At the same time BR removed all facing lock bars and provided 13 new track circuits, while the

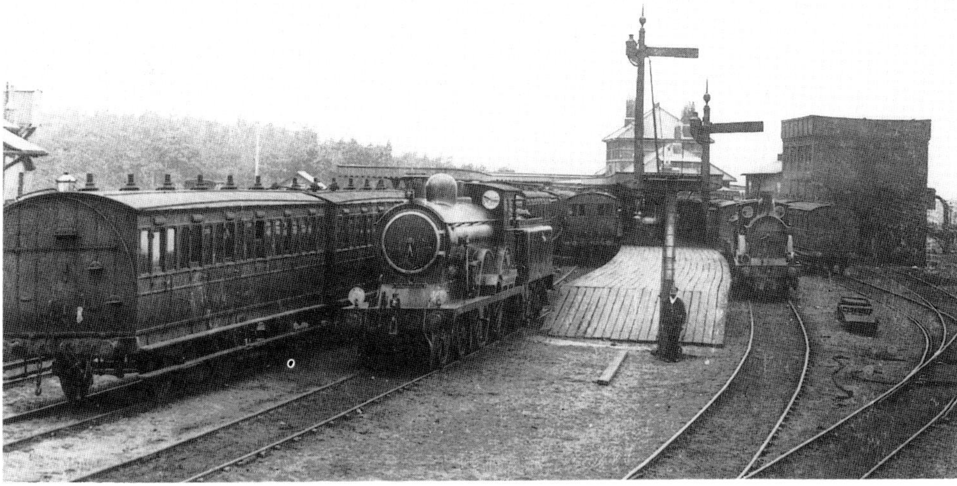

An oil-fired GER 4–4–0 backs onto its train at Cromer. The GER terminus was later designated "Cromer High" to distinguish it from the rival M & GN station at Cromer Beach; note the 2-road locomotive shed with its water tank above. *Lens of Sutton*

An Edwardian view at Cromer GER station (looking north) the flexible hose visible in the foreground was probably used to refill the drinking water tanks provided in restaurant cars. *Lens of Sutton*

A rear view of the main station buildings at Cromer High, taken in July 1954 – just 2 months before this former GER station was closed to passenger traffic. *D. Thompson*

A general view of Cromer High, looking north towards the buffer stops in July 1954. Note that, although three tracks were actually provided, the outer face of the left hand platform could easily have accommodated a fourth terminal road if traffic had justified such a facility. *D. Thompson*

lever frame was enlarged from 29 to 35 levers. Further changes carried out in this comprehensive remodelling included new passenger and parcels facilities, together with the installation of electric lighting throughout the station. The rebuilding was completed on 19th September, 1954, allowing Cromer High to be closed to passenger traffic on the following day.[54]

There is much to see at Cromer. The extensive earthworks and viaducts behind the town are worth viewing on foot, and there are many interesting scenic walks in the vicinity; the cliffs hereabouts rise to 200 ft, and anyone who thinks that "Norfolk is flat" is advised to descend some of the steeper cliff paths.

Cromer High

Enthusiasts will perhaps be keen to examine the site of Cromer High station, but there is, unfortunately, little or nothing left to see, the site of this abandoned Great Eastern terminus having been redeveloped. The one clue to its existence is the presence of Station Road, which is situated in the eastern part of the town at some distance from the present BR station in Holt Road.

When in use, Cromer High had consisted of two, slightly curving platforms, one of which was virtually an island, with a long bay on its east side in addition to the main terminal road. There was an engine release road between the two platforms, with a small goods yard to the west and an engine shed to the east. The main station building was situated at one end of the easternmost platform, and consisted of a two-storey central block with single storey extensions at each end. Extensive, flat-topped Great Eastern canopies covered a considerable part of both platforms, and the entire layout was controlled from a standard GER signal cabin; until 1906 the box had 45 levers but when the line was doubled an enlarged, 70-lever signal box was provided.[55]

To the south of the passenger station, and at some distance from the platforms, a series of parallel carriage sidings were linked to the running lines by a complicated series of crossovers. An interesting feature of the station was the way that the Norfolk & Suffolk Joint line passed beneath the GER complex *en route* from Roughton Road Junction to Mundesley-on-Sea. This low level track bisected the terminus roughly midway between Cromer Junction and the terminal buffers (although there was, of course, no physical connection between the GER and N&S systems).

Cromer High could hardly be described as a large station, but its track layout and signalling arrangements were complex. All three platform roads were signalled for bi-directional working, and this refinement was especially useful during the height of the summer when the station handled a variety of extra trains. To facilitate this method of operation, the terminus was equipped with an impressive array of wooden-posted Great Eastern signals. The towering gantry which carried the station's home arms was a particularly elaborate specimen. Dating from around 1887, it had two main posts and two brackets, and these four "dolls" (posts carrying signal arms) carried three home arms controlling entry to the platforms, two ringed shunting arms (for the goods yard and engine shed respectively), three home signal repeater arms working in conjunction with the main signals, and a characteristic Great Eastern "calling on" signal – which allowed incoming trains to draw forwards into an occupied section at dead slow speed. Additionally, the gantry also supported the Cromer Junction up distant, and there were, as a result, no less than ten working signal arms on one set of posts.[56]

In terms of operation, Cromer High was at a disadvantage when through trains were run from Sheringham to Norwich via the GER line, and in these circumstances it was usual for up trains to stop at Cromer Junction and reverse into the station prior to resuming their southwards journeys. In the down direction, Cromer High portions could be worked into the terminus after stopping at Cromer Junction for Sheringham vehicles to be detached. (The appendix to the May 1942 working timetable reveals that passenger trains "not exceeding ten bogie vehicles" could be propelled from Cromer Junction into the station if piloted by a "competent man").

In its Edwardian heyday, the Great Eastern station provided employment for a considerable number of porters, clerks, signalmen, permanent way men and train crews, and in addition to these directly-employed railway staff, the station created work for a large number of cab drivers – who were needed to convey Edwardian travellers (and mountains of luggage) to and from the station. On summer Saturdays, cabmen were obviously in great demand, and seasoned travellers would make sure that they sat at the front of the train in order to secure a conveyance from the station; passengers from the rear half of the train were often faced with a long walk to their hotels (or a lengthy wait until the cabs returned).

Cromer's station master, from 1877 until around 1898, was Francis Benns, but at the turn-of-the-century the terminus was supervised by James Rowe. Mr Rowe remained at the station for only a few years, and by 1906 he had been replaced by Charles W. Barton.[57] Other employees in the Edwardian period included foreman-porter William Hannant and goods clerk S.W. Barton; the latter (thought to have been the station master's son) emigrated to Canada in about 1912. The station master in the years following World War I was Harry Youell, who had been associated with the Cromer branch for many years, having previously served as station master at North Walsham.

West Runton

Returning to the former Midland & Great Northern station at Cromer Beach, it would now be convenient to resume our journey to Sheringham over the present day branch. Reversing out of Cromer, modern dmus proceed through the cuttings and over another arm of the former triangular junction in order to reach Sheringham.

Running over the only 3¾ miles of the old M&GNR left open in public ownership, the trains reach West Runton in about 3 minutes. This tiny, intermediate stopping place is provided with a boarded-up wooden shack on a single platform. It is a modest place, but one which was served by both

An Edwardian view of West Runton's single platform station; facilities here were utterly basic, and consisted of a small, wood-and-iron station building and a grounded Midland Railway box van; note the glass lanterns, bolted to the front of upright wooden posts rather than on top. *Lens of Sutton*

Another view of West Runton this time looking towards the road bridge and photographed in the British Railways era. *Lens of Sutton*

A further Edwardian view of West Runton this time showing the grounded van and Hotel. *Lens of Sutton*

Cromer Junction with class 'B1', No. 61283 on a Melton Constable freight in August 1961. *H.N. James*

Two views of class 'B1' 4–6–0 No. 61043 at Runton West Junction with a through Melton Constable to Norwich freight in August 1961. West Runton is in the distance (*bottom view*) and the signals indicate that the train will be taking the direct west-to-east curve between Runton West and Newstead Lane junctions. *H.N. James*

Sheringham station, seen from the nearby road overbridge c.1912. Note that, in the absence of proper carriage sidings, spare coaching stock has been shunted into the goods yard. *Real Photographs*

Sheringham station, looking west towards Melton Constable in the Edwardian era; in the left distance, passenger stock can be seen in the goods yard – there being no proper carriage sidings at this busy seaside station. *Lens of Sutton*

Sheringham station in the 1960s. *Lens of Sutton*

Sheringham platform as it is today. *Lens of Sutton*

A view from Sheringham station to the road overbridge and bracket signals.
H.N. James

Sheringham, closed by B.R. in January 1967, is now the headquarters of the North Norfolk Railway; all British Rail trains use a nearby unstaffed halt. *S.C. Jenkins*

An original Derby-lightweight DMU on a local service for Holt seen here at Sheringham in 1959. *Andrew C. Ingram*

Preserved class 'J15' 0–6–0 No. 65462 stands at the platform in Sheringham (North Norfolk) station; these engines first appeared on the Cromer Branch in the 19th Century. *S.C. Jenkins*

the "Broadsman" and the "Norfolkman" named expresses! West Runton has always been a passenger-only station, and no goods facilities were ever provided; its lengthy platform was, however, long enough to cope with summer holiday trains, and there was room for the installation of a second platform and crossing loop if traffic had justified such a facility.

Sheringham

Departing from West Runton, trains follow the coast towards their destination, and, passing beneath the A149, the route enters the outer environs of Sheringham. This attractive seaside resort has, in recent years, started to rival Cromer – although the latter has remained the most important of the two towns. Like Cromer, Sheringham was a railway creation, and its development would not have been possible without the presence of the Midland & Great Northern line which brought large numbers of holidaymakers from the East Midlands and elsewhere.

Sheringham station reflected the town's importance as a significant holiday destination, although the facilities provided here were less complex than those at Cromer Beach or Cromer High. The layout provided three long platform faces, one of which was a dead-end bay whereas the remaining two were through platforms. Incoming excursions were sometimes stabled in the aforementioned bay, but when traffic was especially heavy, spare coaching stock was also accommodated in the adjacent goods sidings.

Erected in 1887, towards the end of the Victorian era, Sheringham's commodious station buildings did not exhibit any particular architectural style. There were no gothic or overtly classical details, and instead the well-built booking offices and waiting rooms were a *tour de force* of purely Victorian architecture – an essay in late 19th century modernity which allowed bricklayers and other craftsmen to show their skills in the use of brick, glass and ironwork. Both platforms were partially covered by extensive canopies, and the up and down sides of the station were linked by a lattice girder footbridge. Also worthy of note was the level crossing that carried a busy street across the running lines at the eastern end of the platforms.

Sadly, this fine Victorian station was superceded by an austerely-simple halt on 2nd January, 1967, but the old station survives as the headquarters of the North Norfolk Railway, which now runs about 3 miles of the M&GN as a preserved railway. Stock movements onto the North Norfolk have given rise to some interesting workings on the Cromer line. On 16th March, 1975, for example, five passenger vehicles and a van were taken to Cromer behind a class '31', then, as there is no run round loop at Sheringham (BR) the big diesel propelled its train along the 3¾ miles of single line to Sheringham. On arrival the stock was shunted into the North Norfolk station over a temporary connection laid by volunteers.

Before leaving Sheringham, it is interesting to reflect that this M&GN station was used as a "terminus" by Great Eastern services which, after July 1906, were able to reach the Midland & Great Northern system via Cromer Junction and Newstead Lane junction. Two GER drivers and two firemen

An old postcard view of Overstrand station, note the subway leaving the platform and level crossing. *J. Kite*

A view of Overstrand station showing the substantial station buildings and also entrance to the sloping subway. *Lens of Sutton*

The final view of Overstrand station shows the diminutive GNR style signal box situated on the platform. *Lens of Sutton*

The wooden platform of the Cromer Links Halt is seen in this early view. Note the non-existence of any station building or weather protection for the waiting passengers. *Lens of Sutton*

were based at Sheringham to work these through services, but, apart from a mess room and engine inspection pit, there were no facilities for Great Eastern locomotives or train crews.

Cromer Links Halt

Having examined the present "main line" between Norwich, Cromer and Sheringham, we must now retrace our steps to Roughton Road Junction in order to study the route and architecture of the Mundesley line in greater detail. (It is necessary at this point to change from the present to the past tense, because the former Norfolk & Suffolk Joint line between Roughton Road Junction and North Walsham has been closed and lifted for many years).

Commencing their journeys at Cromer Beach, Mundesley "locals" followed the path taken by present day trains as far as Roughton Road Junction, from where the Norfolk & Suffolk Joint line continued due west through Cromer Tunnel. With a length of only 61 yds, this was a very modest piece of civil engineering, but the tunnel was of particular interest in that it was one of only two anywhere in Norfolk – the other being at Barsham on the Wells-next-the-Sea branch. However, Barsham Tunnel disappeared around the time that Cromer Tunnel was built – in the words of *The Great Eastern Railway Magazine* it was opened-out "a few years before" 1912 – and with the removal of this earlier tunnel, Cromer Tunnel became the *only* tunnel in Norfolk.!

Emerging onto the first of many embankments *en route* to Mundesley, the bustling 'F4' or 'F6' 2–4–2Ts soon reached Cromer Links Halt. Opened in 1923, this simple, unstaffed halt consisted of a short wooden platform, with a large nameboard and two wooden seats. No shelter was provided, and the sleeper-built platform was supported by wooden trestles.

Overstrand

From Cromer Links, the single line fell towards Overstrand on a 1 in 100 gradient. Situated some 4 miles 24 chains from Cromer Beach, Overstrand was an unusual station, and one that was, in many ways, out-of-place in East Anglia. Its track layout consisted of an 18 chain passing loop, with a central island platform and a small goods yard on the up side. Pedestrian access was by means of a low-level underpass or subway, from which a long covered ramp ascended in unexpected fashion. The subway was too narrow to permit the passage of road traffic, and for this reason there was a level crossing for road vehicles using the lane between Overstrand village and nearby Northrepps.

The platform was 500 ft in length, and the extensive station buildings would have been appropriate at a main line station. Of brick construction, they contained the usual booking office, staff accommodation, waiting rooms and toilets. Unusually, one end of the single storey building was gabled, whereas the other end had a pitched roof; moreover, canopies were provided at only one end, leaving roughly one half of the structure looking rather bare and unfinished. It is likely that the building was designed to

No. 62523 arriving at Trimingham station with the 1.25 pm Cromer Beach to North Walsham service in May 1953.
H.N. James

An M & GN notice at Trimingham – elsewhere, there were identical notices bearing the initials N & SJR.
H.N. James

A derelict Trimingham station in Norwich 1963. *D. Thompson*

A further view of No. 62523 at Trimingham station in 1953. *H.N. James*

facilitate rapid extension if holiday traffic had built-up in the years following opening – though, as we have seen, such an extension was never needed because the hoped-for traffic simply failed to appear.

A single storey signal cabin was sited on one end of the platform, and like other Norfolk & Suffolk boxes, the structure was of GNR, rather than Great Eastern appearance. No goods shed was provided, although a small uncovered loading dock was available to deal with general merchandise traffic.

A visitor, arriving at Overstrand for the first time, would have been surprised to see the picturesque scenery visible on either side of the line, and with its wooded hills and steep cliffs, "Poppyland" did not appear to be part of the "flat" East Anglia of popular imagination. "The scenery here", wrote V.L. Whitechurch in 1898, "is wildly romantic; the coast is girt with lofty, cragged cliffs, and indented by a deep ravine, through which a small rivulet flows into the sea. Notwithstanding this, its firm and smooth sands cannot be surpassed for safe and excellent bathing at all times of the tide". A few years earlier, Clement Scott had wandered from the comparatively developed resort of Cromer to find peace and solitude on the high cliffs further east:

> It was the rule to go on the sands in the morning, to walk on one cliff for a mile in the afternoon, to take another mile in the opposite direction at sunset, and to crowd upon the little pier at night. But the limit went the other way. No one thought of going beyond the lighthouse; that was the boundary of all investigation. Outside that marked the country, the farms and the villages were as lonely as the Highlands.[58]

Sidestrand Halt

It was because of Clement Scott's writings that the Mundesley to Cromer line was built, and the appreciative traveller, having read about "Poppyland" prior to his visit, would not have been disappointed as his train ambled south eastwards along the coast towards Sidestrand Halt. For dedicated seekers of "Poppyland", this was perhaps the highlight of the entire journey, for here, where a "tower in ruins" stood "guard o'er the deep", Clement Scott had composed *The Garden of Sleep*. Sadly, the ruined tower of St Michael's Church was destroyed by a cliff fall in 1916. Sidestrand Halt was, like its counterpart at Cromer Links, a simple wooden platform; opened to the public on 25th May, 1936, it could accommodate just one coach and all tickets were issued on the trains.

Trimingham

Leaving Sidestrand, the railway dropped at 1 in 100, and with the sea less than half a mile to the north, trains approached Trimingham (6 miles 56 chains). This station was similar to neighbouring Overstrand, with an 18 chain passing loop and a central island platfrom, topped by the same brick-built offices and waiting rooms. As at Overstrand, the station building was provided with a sort of "half-length" platform canopy, but in this case access was from a nearby overbridge rather than via a subway.

Rationalisation of facilities had commenced as early as 1922 when the signal box was taken out of use, but the loop was not immediately lifted, and up and down signals remained in place – albeit marked with large crosses to show that they were not in use. It is possible that this rationalisation was initially conceived as a temporary measure, but when it became clear that traffic would not materialise at this remote place, the former down running line was lifted, leaving only the up line in place beside the deserted platform.

Departing from Trimingham, branch trains rumbled beneath the overbridge at the eastern end of the station, and with the 226 ft Beacon Hill prominent to the left, the 2–4–4Ts and their vintage coaches continued towards Mundesley-on-Sea. Having surmounted a miniature "summit" at Sidestrand the railway ran downhill for several miles, with gradients of 1 in 180 beyond Trimingham, steepening in one place to 1 in 100. Nearing Mundesley, the descent eased to 1 in 165 before the route turned sharply to the right on the approaches to Mundesley-on-Sea station.

Mundesley-on-Sea

Mundesley-on-Sea was the principal intermediate station on the Cromer to North Walsham coastal route, and unlike Overstrand and Trimingham, the village did enjoy modest growth after the opening of the railway. With its miniature promenade and ornamental gardens, Mundesley-on-Sea had many of the attributes of a successful seaside resort, and although not as busy as Cromer or Sheringham, Mundesley attracted an appreciable number of satisfied holidaymakers – many of whom returned for year after year.

The station, situated some 9 miles 22 chains from Cromer Beach and 5 miles 3 chains from North Walsham, boasted three lengthy through platforms and a dead-end bay, together with a commodious goods yard on the up side. There was also a two road engine shed which, according to the 1919 GER "system map", was able to accommodate two small tank engines of the 'M15', or similar, type.

The main station buildings were on the up side, and there was a corresponding range of buildings on the opposite platform, which was an island with tracks on either side. Both buildings were equipped with commodious canopies, and the main building sported a curious raised cupola; the up and down platforms were connected by a lattice girder footbridge. Other facilities at this well-laid out station included a cattle dock, loading bays and two Great Northern-style signal cabins, designated Mundesley North and Mundesley South. In 1930, the North box was abolished and points at the northern end of the station were adapted for motor operation from the former South box; the nearby engine shed had, by that time, already been removed.

In its declining years Mundesley-on-Sea station was used as a convenient storage place for spare coaching stock, and it was also a parking place for a rake of camping coaches that were, at one time, parked in the seldom-used loop platform. These vehicles were rented by members of the public who cooked and slept aboard the coaches while using the nearby station for supplies of fresh water and toilet facilities.

Two fine views of the elegant station (with clock tower) at Mundesley-on-Sea showing the girder footbridge and ornate glass platform canopy. *Real Photographs*

Paston and Knapton station with its large station buildings seen here in November 1963. *D. Thompson*

The station buildings at Paston and Knapton photographed when new, showing the elegant design incorporating the station master's house and station facilities. *Oakwood Collection*

In common with other joint systems, the Norfolk & Suffolk line had its "own" staff, who seldom transferred to the parent companies; in earlier days Norfolk & Suffolk employees apparently wore distinctive dark green uniforms with silver buttons, and this may have contributed to a distinct "family" atmosphere at Mundesley and the other N&S stations. One of the first station masters here was Thomas Murrell, who was in office in 1904 but had been replaced, during World War I, by a Mr Moulton. Later, in the years following the Great War, Mundesley's station master was J.E. Summers.

Paston & Knapton

From Mundesley trains ran due south, and with the village of Paston away to the left, the line climbed briefly at 1 in 162 before descending towards the tiny wayside station at Paston & Knapton (11 miles from Cromer). A single platform stopping place, Paston & Knapton had no crossing loop or signal box; its track layout consisted of two dead-end goods sidings, entered via a headshunt on the up side of the line. The station buildings were a miniature version of those at Mundesley, although this similarity was not apparent to the casual observer because, at Paston, one of the two cross wings was raised to a full two storeys in order to provide domestic accommodation for the station master and his family.

Despite its simplicity, Paston & Knapton was, arguably, one of the most attractive stations in the Cromer area, and its rural charm was accentuated by the close proximity of Knapton village. Knapton parish church was clearly visible to the west of the railway, and visitors with an interest in architecture could easily walk the short distance between station and village to see the church's famous double hammer-beam roof.

Beyond Paston & Knapton, the route undulated towards North Walsham, the steepest gradient being a short stretch of 1 in 73. After about one-and-a-half miles, the railway was carried across the derelict North Walsham & Dilham Canal on a single-span bridge. Representing an early attempt to bring improved inland transport to the North Walsham area, this little-known waterway was, in effect, a continuation of the River Ant from Wayford Bridge to Antingham. Opened on 29th August, 1826, the canal was 8¾ miles long, and there were several locks *en route* to the head of navigation at Antingham. North Walsham was the only "large" town served by the canal – Dilham being reached by a detached waterway that branched westwards from the River Ant. The coming of the railway effectively killed the North Walsham canal, and its northernmost extremity was abandoned as early as the 1890s; further damage was caused by the disastrous floods of 1912, and the last wherry left North Walsham in December 1934. Parts of the derelict waterway remained accessible to small pleasure craft, and the River Ant is, happily, still fully navigable.[59]

Having crossed the North Walsham & Dilham Canal, the branch continued south-westwards to Antingham Road Junction, where the route forked; to the left, a line diverged in order to reach the Midland & Great Northern station at North Walsham Town, while to the right, a double track spur continued south westwards for a short distance before joining the East Norfolk branch at North Walsham Junction. The converging lines at this point were originally controlled by a junction box with 20 levers, but in the mid-1920s this box was abolished, and in its place the junction was worked by motor points worked from North Walsham's main signal box.

Sources for Chapter 6

52 *The Railway Times*, 26th September 1874.
53 PRO MT6 files
54 *The Railway Magazine*, March 1954 p.212
55 PRO MT6 files.
56 J.N. Maskelyne, A Remarkable Signal Gantry, *Model Railway News*, September 1950 p.177
57 *The Great Eastern Railway Magazine*, 1912; *Kellys Directory of Norfolk*.
58 Clement Scott, *"Poppyland Papers"*.
59 Alan Faulkner, Broadland Background, *Waterways World*, May 1979 pp.38–44.

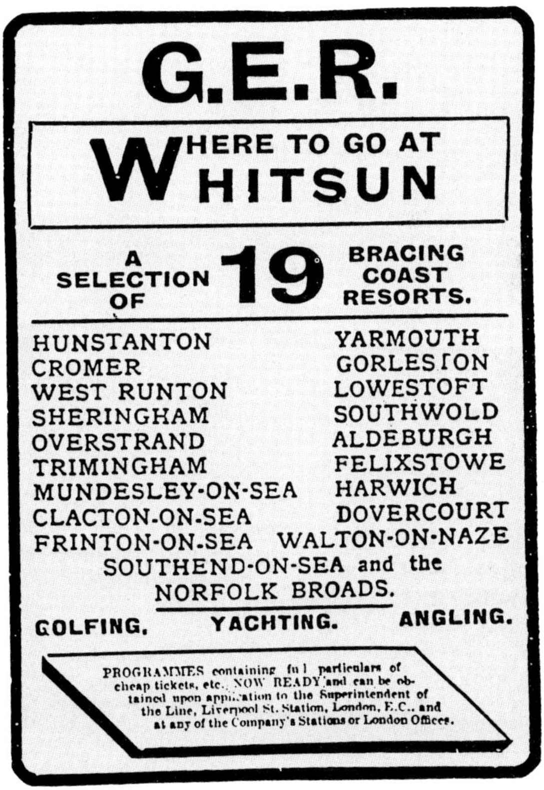

Chapter Seven

Miscellaneous Details

The East Norfolk line and its branches to Mundesley and Sheringham have undergone many changes in the years since they were opened to traffic, and in addition to major rebuildings associated with doubling in the 1890s and rationalisation in the 1960s, there have been countless smaller changes in terms of minor details. Such matters cannot easily be fitted into a coherent narrative, and it seems sensible to conclude with a chapter of miscellaneous details. Many of these relate to the physical appearance of the Cromer, Sheringham and Mundesley lines, and it is hoped that this final section will be of particular interest to potential modellers as well as general readers. (The station details should be read in conjunction with the previous chapter, and studied in relation to the photographs accompanying that section).

Station Architecture

Victorian architecture has often been (unfairly) criticised because of its alleged over-ornamentation, but critics of the Victorian age usually overlook the fact that modern architecture had its roots in the 19th century, and many late Victorian architects actually disliked overt detail or ornament. Among these so-called "modernists" was Norman Shaw, who perfected a domestic style of archtecture characterised by use of "vernacular" features such as chimneys, gables and mullions. Perhaps fortuitously, this type of late-Victorian architecture found much favour on both the Great Eastern *and* Midland & Great Northern railways, and most stations on the Cromer line or on its branches exhibited vernacular revival features.

Before describing these late Victorian buildings it is necessary to remember that East Norfolk architecture was of the pre-fabricated variety, and Salhouse, Wroxham and Worstead all had simple, wooden buildings constructed of what seem to have been standard components. The resulting buildings were more complex than might be imagined, particularly when – as in the case of Wroxham – a change of level was involved.

In time, these earlier stations became inadequate, and at a time of growing traffic the Great Eastern provided subsidiary accommodation at Salhouse, Wroxham and Worstead. At North Walsham (which probably resembled the other stations when first built) the old East Norfolk buildings were removed altogether and in their place the GER erected new offices and waiting rooms on both up and down platforms.

The subsidiary buildings at Salhouse, Wroxham and Worstead were built in the same style as the new buildings at North Walsham – all four stations having the "Norman Shaw type" architecture referred to above. Similar, or substantially-similar buildings appeared all over the Great Eastern system in the late Victorian period, and all seem to have been designed by the company's own architect Mr W.N. Ashbee (who also designed the new terminal buildings at Norwich Thorpe). All of the Cromer branch buildings had steeply-pitched roof structures, tall chimneys, and projecting platform canopies, the latter being, in most cases, supported by cast pillars. Like most

Great Eastern canopies, those on the Cromer branch were adorned with intricate fretwork which (on closer examination) varied from station to station.

At Salhouse and Worstead the company fitted standard canopies to the hitherto canopy-less ENR buildings, and as a result of these late Victorian additions the old East Norfolk station buildings were given a deceptively "GER style" appearance. The new canopies were bolted direct to the wooden façades of the two buildings, although, to obtain a neater finish and enhanced strength, vertical timber laths were first attached to the walls in order to receive the cast metal spandrels. Gunton station, meanwhile, needed less work to bring it up to late Victorian traffic requirements, although Gunton did receive a standard GER waiting room on its up platform.

Cromer was progressively improved throughout the Great Eastern period. When opened it had just one platform with tracks on either side, but in or around 1887 the terminus was enlarged by the addition of a new platform to the west of the original. Interestingly, this new platform was designed as an *island*, but in the event the outer, or western-most track was never laid, and for the rest of its working life the station had just three platform faces. In addition to its extra platform, Cromer also received a set of standard GER canopies.

As might be expected, Eastern & Midlands/M&GN architecture owed nothing to Great Eastern practice or traditions, but Cromer Beach and the other M&GN stations were near-contemporaries of their GER counterparts, and for this reason they were also strongly influenced by "vernacular revival" fashions. Cromer, the most elaborate of these M&GN stations, incorporated a bewildering variety of architectural styles, including brick, stone, and "Tudoresque" timber-framing. Some of the spaces between its timber-frames were filled by "brick-nogging" – in other words bricks were used in conjunction with wooden structural members to produce a decorative, and very strong type of walling.

Signalling and Signal Cabins

In the early days of railways, signalling – especially on branch lines – was of a rudimentary nature, with hand-worked signals and pointwork unprotected by mechanical safeguards of any kind. By the 1870s, however, signalling systems had reached a level of sophistication that would, within the next few years, result in a virtually-foolproof system of fully inter-locked signals and pointwork.

The Cromer branch, having been opened at a relatively late date, was fully equipped with signal boxes and semaphore signals from its inception, and most of the intermediate stations had small signal boxes, together with home and distant signals. The latter were, in common with those on other lines, painted red instead of the later, and more familiar, yellow.

The final years of the 19th century witnessed many improvements, and in these years the branch was equipped with signalling of a more complex nature than had originally been provided. At Cromer, for instance, a strategically-placed crossover at the station throat enabled two-way working to be introduced, and it is thought that the elaborate bracket signals referred to in *Chapter Six* were erected around 1887. Cromer was, in those days, still a single-platform terminus with one long platform and a shorter bay, but by 1904 the station had been given a third platform face, with a consequent increase of signal arms and ground discs.

In 1906, the opening of a double track section between Cromer Junction and Cromer station had led to a still more complex signalling system, and for the next sixty years the branch was fully-signalled, with at least one signal box at each station.

The following table shows every signal box on the branch, together with details of the size and make of their level frames; it should be noted that even minor track alterations could result in levers being taken out of use, and for that reason the actual number of levers *in use* at any one time could vary considerably. Nevertheless, the number of levers quoted will give an idea of the relative size of each box.

TABLE 2: DETAILS OF SIGNAL BOXES

Box	*Levers*	*Type of Frame*	*Notes*
Cromer	70	McKenzie & Holland	
Cromer Jn.	43	McKenzie & Holland	installed after 1906 doubling
Gunton	24	McKenzie & Holland	abolished January 1967
North Walsham Jn.	20	McKenzie & Holland	abolished c.1927
North Walsham	41	McKenzie & Holland	
Worstead	25	McKenzie & Holland	
Wroxham Yard	20	McKenzie & Holland	
Wroxham Station	50	McKenzie & Holland	
Salhouse	20	McKenzie & Holland	abolished July 1966
Whitlingham Jn.	37	Saxby & Farmer	

The boxes themselves were of one basic type, and although the number of levers varied considerably, these gabled boxes were fabricated from 6 ft standardised panels. There were usually four 6 ft bays at ground floor level, with five window frames, each of approximately 5 ft, in the glazed upper floors. North Walsham cabin is a good example of this style of Great Eastern box – an interesting feature, in this case, being a projecting bay at first floor level, which was presumably installed to afford the signalmen a clear view beyond the intervening down station building.

Elsewhere, there was considerable variety in terms of staircases, external catwalks and other details. At Worstead, for instance, the cabin had an unusually-steep roof pitch, while at Wroxham the box was taller than normal, and had an external toilet at first floor level. At Salhouse, the signal box was provided with a brick-built lower storey, although in other respects it conformed to the same overall design as its counterparts at other stations.

Signalling on the Norfolk & Suffolk Joint line between North Walsham and Runton junctions followed Great Northern traditions. A glance at some of the photographs depicted in this book will reveal that the GNR-pattern boxes at Mundesley-on-Sea, Trimingham, Overstrand and Runton West were similar to the Great Eastern signal cabins between Norwich and Cromer High, albeit with differing window arrangements and more-ornate barge boards. Roughton Road Junction was in a class of its own, with a curious, pagoda-type roof structure, while at Cromer Beach the hip-roofed cabin provided in later years was of modern design and construction (the original wooden box at Cromer Beach had been an unusually-tall structure, providing an excellent bird's eye view over the entire station and its approaches).

Great Eastern lower quadrant signals survived for many years on the East Norfolk line, but many were subsequently replaced by LNER or BR upper quadrants on tubular steel posts. The Norfolk & Suffolk Joint line, in contrast, was equipped with Great Northern Railway-style somersault signals.

Platform Furniture

Station fences exhibited a variety of styles and method of construction. In East Norfolk days, platforms were fenced with an unusual type of post-and-rail fence in which the spaces between each upright member were filled with diagonal wooden struts, but in later years this original ENR fencing was removed, and in its place rather "spindly" metal fences were erected. At Gunton, the platform fences were formed of wooden uprights and tubular steel rails, while many stations on the M&GN or Norfolk & Suffolk lines boasted decorative Midland-style "diamond-pattern" fencing.

Platform lighting was equally varied, and there were marked variations between Great Eastern and M&GN practice. Stations on the original East Norfolk line originally had typical Great Eastern style "square lantern" lights – those at Cromer High having decorative posts while their counterparts at most of the smaller stations had simple wooden uprights which were, in many cases,an integral part of the platform fencing. Midland & Great Northern stations, in contrast, were equipped with glass-fronted lanterns that could be attached either to buildings or to upright timber posts; at Cromer Beach, however, ornate gas lights were provided.

Most stations on the Cromer line and its branches were lit by oil lamps, gas being provided only at more important places. Latterly, electric lighting was installed, and in most cases the original wood or metal lamp posts were replaced by tubular steel posts supporting glass lamps of roughly hemispherical appearance. Such lamps were installed at Norwich, Salhouse, Wroxham and Worstead. In a more recent development, BR equipped most of the surviving stations with angular electric lamps that displayed the station name.

In earlier days, many stations had attractive – though possibly rather uncomfortable – platform seats incorporating the station name in raised letters on their backrests. Such platform seats usually sported a cast "GER" monogram between their metal legs.

The Great Eastern and other pre-grouping companies expressed their individuality in countless ways, and until the wholesale rationalisation of recent years, observant travellers could usually guess what former company they were travelling on merely by looking at lamp posts or other station fixtures! Water columns could, however, present something of a problem, especially in East Anglia where there does not seem to have been any one standard design. At North Walsham, for instance, locomotives replenished their tanks from a "GWR-style" mushroom water tank at the north end of the up platform. At Mundesley-on-Sea, however, a water crane on the down side incorporated an unusually-long rotating boom so that it could reach engines standing on either side of the wide island platform.

Station Liveries

The colour schemes used by Victorian railway companies such as the ENR are, inevitably, a matter of speculation, and railway modellers are often faced with a dilemma when deciding which colours or shades to use. On the other hand, Victorian paint technology was unable to provide a wide range of colours suitable for external use, and for this reason the predominate 19th century colours were buff, brown, or a sort of drab holly green. In the mid Victorian period, for example, most British railway locomotives were painted green with chocolate brown frames, while buildings were typically painted in a two-tone colour scheme involving either green or brown, and a contrasting shade of buff or cream. Other, brighter colours, were obtained only with difficulty; carmine, to take one example, was extracted from dried Cochineal Beetle bodies and sold for about 18s. per lb. at a time when dark holly green cost only 6*d*. per lb!

By the end of the 19th century, German scientists had developed a range of much cheaper paints, but the traditional green-and-cream or brown-and-cream colour schemes remained in vogue for most railway or domestic purposes, and in these circumstances it seems reasonable to suggest that East Norfolk structures were probably adorned in those same colours.

Early photographs of Wroxham show that ENR wooden buildings were painted in a light buff or off-white colour, with white windows frames and dark-coloured external framing; by analogy with other companies this dark colour would have been green or brown. Platform canopies at Cromer and elsewhere were also painted in the usual creamy-buff colour, while supporting ironwork was green or brown. These colours remained standard during the Great Eastern period, but the LNER station livery incorporated a lighter shade of green. Blue enamelled signs appeared in the early BR era, while in the late 1960s external woodwork was painted in an off-white colour scheme.

A Note on Tickets

The study of tickets is an interesting but neglected aspect of local railway studies, and it would, therefore, be of interest to make at least passing mention of this subject. In the early days, stations such as Wroxham and Cromer would have issued ordinary Edmondson card tickets bearing the names of issuing stations and destinations, together with dates and serial numbers; such tickets were printed by the Great Eastern printers at Stratford, and it is believed that tickets used on the Cromer branch carried the initials "GER" rather than "ENR" (although this point is by no means clear).

Like other Victorian railways, the Great Eastern made use of a directional colour code. Briefly, tickets issued for journeys in the up direction were coloured yellow, blue or buff for first, second and third class bookings respectively, while in the down direction the corresponding colours were white, pinkish-red and green. Thus, a second class ticket from Salhouse to Cromer would have been red, whereas a first class ticket from North Walsham to Norwich would have been yellow.

Tickets issued for through journeys to St Pancras or other "foreign" stations were further distinguished by the addition of brightly-coloured horizontal stripes. A first class ticket from St Pancras to Cromer, for instance, would have been white with a horizontal orange band, while a third class single in the opposite direction would have been green with a central red stripe.

This complex ticketing system was simplified in later years, one of the first changes being the abolition of GER second class tickets (outside London) from 1st January, 1893. Directional colours were abandoned in 1914, and in its final years the Great Eastern issued plain white or buff tickets. In the 1930s ordinary LNER singles were coloured green, while first class issues were white; third class cheap day returns were buff, and many issues were enlivened by the addition of bright red letters that were superimposed to denote various types of booking. A similar system persisted into the British Railways period – the main innovation being the introduction of a lighter shade of green for third (later second) class tickets. Second class singles from Gunton to Cromer, for example, were coloured green, whereas a first class ticket for the same journey was plain white; returns were overprinted with a red letter "R" on the return portion, while privilege tickets (issued to BR employees or their families) carried the distinguishing letter "P".

Combined river-rail bookings were offered to the public during the summer season, and for these bookings, ordinary, buff-coloured excursion tickets were issued. The front of the tickets carried the legend "trip on the Norfolk Broads by Broads Tours Services Ltd", together with the words "out boat" and "return rail".

Sadly, the de-staffing carried out in 1967 resulted in the disappearance of traditional railway booking offices with their racks full of Edmondson card tickets, and in their place conductor-guards were equipped with bus-type ticket machines issuing flimsy paper tickets. Thereafter, traditional card tickets were used only for certain through bookings from London, Leicester or other main line stations.

While on the subject of tickets and fare collection it is staggering to recall that, as recently as the 1950s, the average BR ticket was charged at the rate of just 1¾ old pence per mile, and in 1956 the single fares from London to Norwich, Mundesley, Cromer and Sheringham were only 18*s.* 1*d.*, 21*s.* 4*d.*, 21*s.* 10*d.* and 22*s.* 6*d.* respectively! In the early 1960s, the single second class fare from Cromer Beach to Gunton was only 1*s.* 6*d.* while for 4*s.* (i.e. 20p) one could travel all the way from Cromer Beach to Norwich, a distance of 26¾ miles.

Sources and Bibliography

Primary sources for the present study included East Norfolk and other Acts, particularly the ENR Acts of 1864, 1869, 1872 and 1878, together with the M&GN Act of 1898. Information on the progress of Bills through Parliament was gleaned from *The Journal of the House of Commons*, while useful details relating to the early history of the branch were obtained from ENR reports published in *The Railway Times* (see, for example, *page 1264* of the 24th September, 1864 edition, and *page 875* of the 11th September, 1875 edition). Other useful primary sources included *Bradshaw's Shareholders Guides*, *Bradshaw's Railway Timetables*, GER, LNER and BR working timetables, *Kelly's Directories of Norfolk*, and notes, letters and articles in *The Railway Magazine*, *Railway World*, *The Railway Modeller*, *The Great Eastern Railway Magazine*, and *The LNER Magazine*.

The following list of books and articles is appended for the benefit of those seeking further information on the Cromer branch and the history of railways in north Norfolk. The presence of a book or article on the list does not necessarily imply that the work has been used as a source, although many of the articles did provide useful minor details of locomotives working etc.

Cecil J. Allen	*The Great Eastern Railway* (1955).
	The Norfolk Coast Express, *Railway World*,January 1967.
	Great Eastern Train Services of 1905, *Railway World*, November 1965.
	British Express Trains No. 4: Eastern & North Eastern Regions (1960).
A.J. Wrottesley	*The Midland & Great Northern Joint Railway.* (1970).
H.C. Casserley	*Britain's Joint Lines* (1968).
R.S. Joby	*Forgotten Railways of East Anglia* (1977).
Donald I. Gordon	*The Regional History of the Railways of Great Britain, Volume V, The Eastern Counties* (1968).
A. Hanson	Poppyland and One Way to It, *Railway Magazine*, 1898
V.R. Webster	Train Working at Cromer, *Railway Magazine*, September 1954.
G.A. Sekon	Railways in Poppyland, *Railway Magazine*, 1904.
E. Tuddenham	The Norfolk & Suffolk Joint, *Railway World*, July 1966.
	The M&GN Route to Cromer, *Railway World*, 1964.
W.W. Bayles	Mundesley to Cromer, *Trains Illustrated*, 1953.
J.F. Gairns	The Norfolk Lines of the London & North Eastern Railway, *Railway Magazine*, February 1929.
David J. Bosher	Norfolk Postscript, *Railway Magazine*, February 1980.
D.W. Winkworth	Belle Trains, *Railway Magazine*, May 1972.
Eric Neave	Pullman Cars on East Coast Lines, *Railway World*, June 1978.
W.R. Jenkinson	The Predecessors of the Great Eastern Railway, *Great Eastern Magazine*, 1913–15.

Stanley C. Jenkins *The Lynn & Hunstanton Railway* (1987).
The Hunstanton Branch, *Railway World*, June 1984.
The Hunstanton Branch, *Railway Modeller*, January 1987.
The Cromer Branch, *Back Track*, Summer 1987.
Cromer Beach, *Railway Modeller*, April 1977.

W.A. Dutt *The Little Guide to Norfolk* (1903).

G. Parry (Ed) *The Maid of the Mill* (1936).

W.J. Gordon *Every-day Life on the Railroad* (1898).

M.J. Clark The Norfolk & Suffolk Joint Railway, *GERS Journal*, June 1980.

J.H. Farrington Melton Constable, *Railway Modeller*, November 1980.

J.N. Maskelyne A Remarkable Signal Gantry, *Model Railway News*, September 1950.

Alan Faulkner Broadland Background, *Waterways World*, May 1979.

E.L. Ahrons Locomotive & Train Working in the Latter Part of the 19th century, *The Railway Magazine*, 1918.
The Locomotives of the GER, *The Locomotive Magazine*, Vols 7–18, 1901–12.

V.L. Whitechurch Cromer, *The Railway Magazine*, June 1898.

Finally, thanks are due to individuals and organisations who have helped in various ways, among them Lens of Sutton, H.N. James, Alan Taylor, H.C. Casserley, G.R. Mortimer, Colin Judge, and the staffs of the University of Leicester Library, the Public Record Office, and the Fleet Air Arm Museum, RNAS Yeovilton (particularly Len Lovell and the research department).

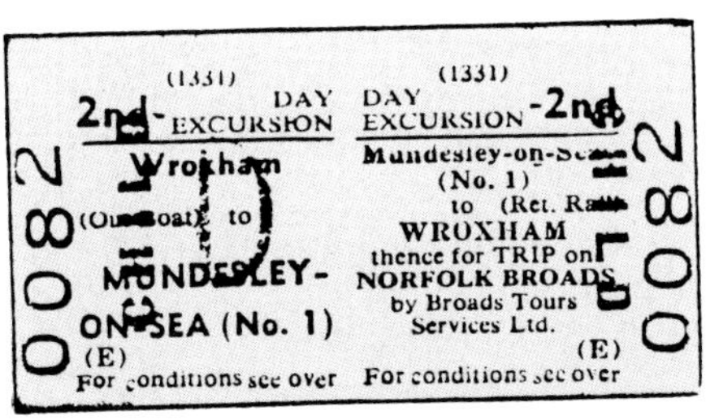

Appendix One

Some Personalities

The East Norfolk Railway was associated with several prominent Victorians, among them Lord Suffield, Charles Thomas Lucas and John Wilson. It may be of interest to conclude with a short *resumé* of their respective careers, and the following biographical notes have therefore been appended to the main text.

Lord Suffield (*1830–1914*): The fifth baron Suffield was a prime supporter of the East Norfolk scheme who contributed both money and (perhaps more importantly) the land on which the railway was built; he was also instrumental in the subsequent development of Cromer.

Charles Thomas Lucas (*1820–95*): Originally an East Anglian building contractor, Charles Thomas Lucas later joined his brother Thomas to form the firm of Lucas Brothers, which carried out many railway building contracts including the East Norfolk line. In 1874 Lucas Brothers joined forces with John Aird & Sons to form the famous Lucas & Aird partnership – although the two firms continued to act independently as and when necessary.

John Wilson: John "Jack" Wilson was a nephew of Edmund Wilson, who had been employed as the ENR Engineer. John played an important part during the building of the ENR, and later carried out much work for the Great Eastern Railway. He died in 1910, and a short tribute appeared on page 229 of the 1922 *Great Eastern Railway Magazine*.

Clement Scott (1841–1904): A writer, and reporter for the *Daily Telegraph*, Clement Scott coined the term "Poppyland" and was thereby instrumental in putting Cromer on the Victorian map. His poem *The Garden of Sleep* became a popular 19th century song when it was set to music by Isodore de Lara, and many people travelled to Sidestrand in order to see the original "Garden of Sleep".

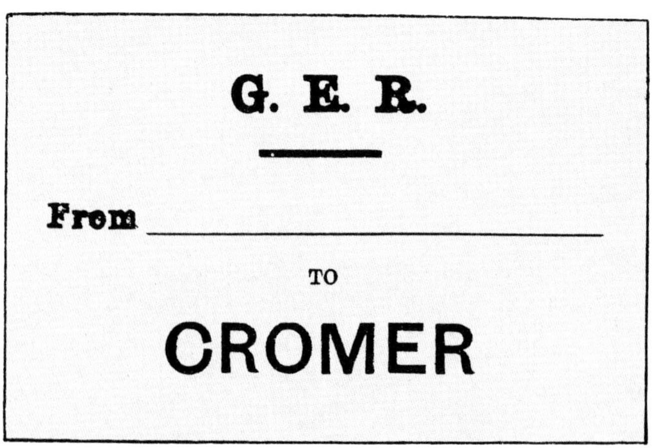

Appendix Two

Great Eastern Station Masters on the ENR Line

Station	*1888*	*1896*	*1904*
Cromer	Francis Benns	Francis Benns	James Rowe
Gunton	William Taylor	James Atkins	James Atkins
N. Walsham	Robert Taylor	Robert Taylor	Robert Taylor
Worstead	Frederick Avery	Frederick Avery	Frederick Avery
Wroxham	Francis Underhill	Francis Underhill	Francis Underhill
Salhouse	George Smith	Charles Notley	William Smith

Station	*1908*	*1912*	*1922*
Cromer	Charles Barton	Charles Barton	Harry Youell
Gunton	Edward Mallott	Edward Mallott	–
N. Walsham	Henry Youell	Henry Youell	–
Worstead	Henry Avery	Henry Avery	Robert Simpson
Wroxham	Francis Underhill	Francis Underhill	Robert Lawrence
Salhouse	William Smith	William Smith	Caleb Impson

Index

Golfing on the East Coast
Yachting on the Norfolk
Angling Broads
TRAVEL IN COMFORT
BY THE
SHERINGHAM
CROMER
OVERSTRAND
MUNDESLEY
YARMOUTH
GORLESTON
LOWESTOFT
SOUTHWOLD
The
Shortest
and
Fastest
Route.
HUNSTANTON
ALDEBURGH
FELIXSTOWE
CLACTON-ON-SEA
FRINTON-ON-SEA
WALTON-ON-NAZE
DOVERCOURT
HARWICH
FAST TRAINS
RESTAURANT CARS.
Saturday to Monday Tickets.
Tourist, Fortnightly and Week-End Tickets.
Cheap Residential Season Tickets.
Write to the Superintendent of the Line, Liverpool Street Station, London, E.C., who will forward, gratis, Descriptive Illustrated Guides, also Pamphlets containing full particulars.